HOPE IN THE LIBRARY

HOPE IN THE LIBRARY

How Libraries Can Help Shape Our Future with Artificial Intelligence

Michael J. Paulus, Jr.

BLOOMSBURY ACADEMIC

NEW YORK • LONDON • OXFORD • NEW DELHI • SYDNEY

BLOOMSBURY ACADEMIC

Bloomsbury Publishing Inc, 1359 Broadway, New York, NY 10018, USA
Bloomsbury Publishing Plc, 50 Bedford Square, London, WC1B 3DP, UK
Bloomsbury Publishing Ireland, 29 Earlsfort Terrace, Dublin 2, D02 AY28, Ireland

BLOOMSBURY, BLOOMSBURY ACADEMIC and the Diana logo are trademarks of Bloomsbury Publishing Plc

First published in the United States of America 2026

Copyright © Michael J. Paulus, Jr., 2026

For legal purposes the List of Illustrations on p. x and Acknowledgments on p. 147 constitute an extension of this copyright page.

Cover design by Darren Rumney / rumneydesign.co.uk
Cover images: Melbourne State library of Victoria © Eric Yang / Getty Images; Abstract digital © Yuichiro Chino / Getty Images

All rights reserved. No part of this publication may be: i) reproduced or transmitted in any form, electronic or mechanical, including photocopying, recording or by means of any information storage or retrieval system without prior permission in writing from the publishers; or ii) used or reproduced in any way for the training, development or operation of artificial intelligence (AI) technologies, including generative AI technologies. The rights holders expressly reserve this publication from the text and data mining exception as per Article 4(3) of the Digital Single Market Directive (EU) 2019/790.

Bloomsbury Publishing Inc does not have any control over, or responsibility for, any third-party websites referred to or in this book. All internet addresses given in this book were correct at the time of going to press. The author and publisher regret any inconvenience caused if addresses have changed or sites have ceased to exist, but can accept no responsibility for any such changes.

A catalog record for this book is available from the Library of Congress.

ISBN:	HB:	979-8-7651-3619-5
	PB:	979-8-7651-3618-8
	ePDF:	979-8-7651-3621-8
	eBook:	979-8-7651-3622-5

Typeset by Integra Software Services Pvt. Ltd.
Printed and bound in the United States of America

For product safety related questions contact productsafety@bloomsbury.com.

To find out more about our authors and books visit www.bloomsbury.com and sign up for our newsletters.

To Mike and Sally Paulus, 1936–2025,
for giving me a love of learning,
and to the Gig Harbor Library,
for providing me a place of rest as my parents entered theirs.

CONTENTS

List of Illustrations x

PART ONE PROLOGUES: REVISITING THE MEANING AND PURPOSE OF LIBRARIES IN AN AGE OF AI 1

0 On Order 3
1 Portals to Hope 9
2 Pandemic 13
3 Becoming a Librarian 17
4 Why Libraries? 21

PART TWO THE LIBRARY AS AN ARCHIVE: HOW LIBRARIES ARE SOURCES OF HOPE 25

5 The Emergence of Attention and Imagination 27
6 Living Libraries 30
7 The City 33
8 The Beginning of the Book 36
9 The Beginning of the Library 40
10 The End of a Library 44

11 The Library as a Transformative Technology 47
12 The Industrial Imagination 51
13 Archival Fevers 54
14 On Inexactitude in Libraries 57

PART THREE THE LIBRARY AS A SITE OF ANTICIPATION: HOW LIBRARIES ARE SIGNS OF HOPE 61

15 The Antilibrary 63
16 The Apocalyptic Imagination 67
17 Libraries of Babylon 70
18 Libraries of New Atlantis 75
19 Promethean Hopes 78
20 A Canticle for Libraries 81
21 Facing the End with Libraries 84
22 Library 2041 87
23 Trusting a Future Library 91
24 The Postdigital Library 94

PART FOUR THE LIBRARY AS A PLACE OF ACTION: HOW LIBRARIES ARE STRUCTURES FOR HOPE 99

25 The Library at Dawn 101
26 The Archival Cycle 104

27 The Future of the Book 109
28 The New Media Library 112
29 Library Automation and Intelligence Augmentation 116
30 From Alexandria to Alexa—and Back 119
31 The Library and Virtue 123
32 In and Beyond Buildings 128
33 On Enduring Institutions 131
34 Finding Oneself in the Library 135

PART FIVE END MATTERS 139

35 After the End 141

Acknowledgments 147
Bibliographic Essay 150
Topical Pathways and Explorations 162
Index 167

ILLUSTRATIONS

Figures

1.1 The 10th-Floor Reading Room of the Central Branch of the Seattle Public Library, 2022 (photographed by the author) 8
8.1 The Library of Ashurbanipal on Display in the British Museum, used with permission 37
14.1 Sources Continuum. Diagram by the author 59
17.1 Vancouver (BC) Public Library's Central Branch, 2023, which regularly appears in sci-fi shows (photographed by the author) 74
26.1 The Book Lifecycle. Diagram by the author 105
26.2 The Records Lifecycle. Diagram by the author 106
26.3 The Archival Cycle. Diagram by the author 107
26.4 The Archival Cycle. Diagram by the author 108
33.1 Duke Humphrey's Library, Oxford University, 2022 (photographed by the author) 134
35.1 Inside the Central Branch of the Birmingham Library, 2022 (photographed by the author) 145

Tables

31.1 IAV Framework. Table by the author 125
31.2 Applying the IAV Framework. Table by the author 126

PART ONE

PROLOGUES: REVISITING THE MEANING AND PURPOSE OF LIBRARIES IN AN AGE OF AI

A   General Works

0 ON ORDER

In the Library of Congress, in Washington, D.C., there is a permanent exhibition of Thomas Jefferson's library. More precisely, what is displayed in one of the building's great marble pavilions is a re-creation of one of Jefferson's personal libraries—the one he sold to Congress to reestablish the library destroyed when British soldiers sacked Washington in 1814. The books, encased on shelves forming a spiral, are arranged under three categories: history, philosophy, and fine arts. Jefferson's classification scheme follows one proposed some two hundred years earlier by Francis Bacon, who organized knowledge into what he considered to be the primary faculties of the mind used in studying various subjects: memory for history, reason for philosophy and science, and imagination for creative works. For Bacon, the world was like a set of books and all our cognitive capabilities are required to understand what is revealed in them.

Asked to assess these approaches to organizing knowledge, a generative AI model noted how they resonate with patterns of human cognition—how we remember the past, reason about the present, and imagine the future. When asked how it would organize knowledge, the model described more dynamic, multifaceted, personalized, and predictive methods for accessing information. This approach would create an optimized classification that would cohere, momentarily, for the immediate need of the prompter. Relevant bits of books and other media—or, more likely, simple summaries of them—would emerge for temporary use. In such a highly personalized and efficient system, human judgment is displaced by statistical means, cultural and contextual differences are generalized, and people are separated both from the sources of knowledge they are accessing as well as how others are accessing them. All of this automated classification of data is performed without anything like human experience, understanding, or imagination. This approach and analysis can be helpful and insightful, but overdependence on computational capabilities could limit what and how we remember, narrow our engagement with the present, and replace imagined possibilities with statistically probable outcomes. But AI can provide us with a new, different, and supplemental way of reading actual books as well as Bacon's figurative books of the world.

Centuries before Bacon, Augustine of Hippo—one of the most prominent readers and writers of antiquity—linked reading and understanding with our experience of time. Time, Augustine said, is present to us in three ways: in the presence of past things, in the presence of present things, and in the presence of future things. Each sense of time engages a different dimension of temporal awareness: the past is present through memory, the present is present through direct perception, and the future is present through expectation. To illustrate how the mind organizes these experiences of time, Augustine describes the process of reciting a poem. The recitation begins with the text existing in expectation. During the recitation, the attention and actions of the speaker are divided between parts already and not yet recited. Until the end, action is shaped by memory and expectation. Augustine said this experience of reciting a text—of expectation becoming memory through attention and action—can be extended to an individual's life and to human history. Even when the end of the text, or a life, or all of human history is unknown, reading and thinking involve anticipating what may come next and directing our actions responsively.

We experience reality, and discover and create meaning with others in the world, through shared recollections, imagining, and reasoning. For millennia, we have depended on books and the libraries that provide access to them to extend what we know and experience—not only as individuals, but throughout societies. Beyond the years of one life or the decades of a family's survival, libraries measure time at the scale of centuries and millennia. To cultivate a full experience of human temporality—encounters with time that transcend the fragmented and fleeting experiences of individual lives—libraries preserve and create memories of the past, expectations of the future, and present understandings of the world. To encounter a library is to engage with archives of the past, anticipations about the future, and agency for action in the present. This keeping of attention is always for some end, to form a particular type of person or culture. These hoped-for ends may be limited and flawed, as when libraries become tools of oppressive empires or governments. But the human agency facilitated by libraries can and does enable the realization of better and greater hopes.

This book is about these core functions of the library—as an archive, as a site of anticipation, and as a place of action—and why this unique institution remains especially important in the age of artificial intelligence. Libraries are our archives of the past; what we know about the past we know largely because there have been and are libraries preserving memories of who we have been and what we have done. Presuming that there will be people in the future interested in such things, libraries are created and sustained for people yet unborn and societies not yet formed. Libraries also are our archives of possible futures, preserving both practical and radical visions of who we might become and of alternative worlds we may create and inhabit. In organizing information for and about the future, libraries become sources of hope. Even in our darkest apocalyptic imaginings, libraries persist as sites and signs of anticipation—not just about the end of the world as we know it, but about the purposes of human existence and the possibilities of human potential. Most concretely, libraries exist as structures that connect past knowledge and future anticipations to enable action in the present. These are ancient functions of libraries, but they have become even more crucial as we have become increasingly dependent on automated information processing. Our world is being filled with and redesigned for artificial agents, which are transforming how we discover, engage with, and create information. Artificial and automated intelligence is being integrated into libraries, augmenting how we process, discover, and use information. But the library—as a human-centered infrastructure and a human-scaled interface for our information environment—has a vital role in cultivating human hopes and agency within this emerging environment.

There are those who argue that, given the power and potential of AI, human-curated libraries will or should be superseded. This is an old argument, predictably made when a powerful new technology such as the personal computer or the internet appears. Against such innovations libraries are perceived as too limited and flawed, expensive and inefficient, slow to change and unsustainable. These criticisms can be made of the new technologies themselves, especially AI systems. Shannon Vallor describes AI systems as inadequate mirrors. AI presents fixed and reductive representations of reality, but reality is open and surprising. We are, therefore, "endlessly making ourselves anew." We do learn from predictable patterns, but we learn from surprising anti-patterns as well. And one of the chief things we learn is "that we are beings for whom there is always hope." By itself, AI is an untrusty curator of shared human experiences, understandings, and hopes. Too much is hidden from and inaccessible to AI and it, alone, cannot tell us the story of our past, what is worthy of our attention, and what our responsibilities are. Vallor notes, "there is hope for us to be something more with AI—and with one another—than what we have been." In their book about AI hype, Emily Bender and Alex Hanna call out a more trustworthy and "vital force in our communities": "the practices of libraries, librarians, and library science. These are the places to look for deeply informed ideas and practices around what it means for information access to be a public good." Libraries and librarians have a significant role in and responsibility for leveraging the distinctives of both human and artificial intelligence to realize true hope over false hype.

Through a series of essays, in the tradition of Michel de Montaigne's reflective and explorative *assays*, this book argues that the library, augmented with AI, should continue to function as an enduring source, sign, and structure of hope. Informed by more than two decades of studying and leading libraries, these essays combine insights from personal reflections, professional experience, and original research. Further, they offer a unique synthesis of literature about the history and future of libraries. These essays are organized into four sections. The first, introductory section provides an orientation to the major themes explored throughout the book—the past, future, and present hopes of libraries. The next three sections explore the library in time—through memory and the past, imagination and the future, and actions in the present—to reveal the depth, breadth, and power of the library as an institution for augmenting knowledge. A final section includes a concluding essay, acknowledgment and bibliographic essays, suggested topical pathways through the book meant to encourage further reflection and exploration, and an index of ancient texts, libraries, and people. Each essay in this book also falls under classifications from the current Library of Congress system, to point to the broad range of subjects that concern the library as a human and technological phenomenon. This book can be read from beginning to end, or in any other order a reader may choose. Each essay and section, like a book or division in a library, may be read independently. There is, one hopes, something to be gained by the whole as it is organized into this book. But the whole is never exhaustive, and sometimes parts are sufficient and worthy of independent attention. The main point emphasized throughout this book is that the library is a critical and constructive agent of social and technological transformation in and for our present time. Libraries, through the work of librarians and others who work in them, can help us comprehend, critique, and collaborate with AI to create a better information environment for both human and artificial agents.

To organize a library is to create an ordered view of the world. Reflecting on his attempt to create his own library as an interpretation of reality, Walter Benjamin acknowledged "the dialectical tension between the poles of disorder and order" in the life of a library builder. Human schemes of order are artificial and provisional, sometimes helpful but often harmful. Knowledge transcends our attempts to attain and contain it, but our flawed systems are capable of helping us grow in knowledge and wisdom if they our open, adaptive, and our ultimate ends are not constrained by them. Throughout their history, libraries have been both open and oppressive systems. Yet, through flawed attempts at organizing and disseminating knowledge, they have revealed alternative and deeper orders—perspectives previously ignored, excluded, and unknown as well as new and emerging ones. The essays in this book point to ways libraries have been and are being created to realize a better future as humanity continues to evolve and develop along with our latest artificial creations. Libraries can help us augment AI as it augments us.

FIGURE 1.1 The 10th-Floor Reading Room of the Central Branch of the Seattle Public Library, 2022 (photographed by the author)

1 PORTALS TO HOPE

When the Seattle Public Library began planning for a twenty-first-century replacement of its mid-twentieth-century Central Library facility, planners identified three major challenges that needed to be addressed with a new building. First, what would be the place of legacy print materials? Second, how should space be shaped for new and emerging technologies? And, finally, what types of spaces do library patrons need now? These three questions concern the past, future, and present of every library. How do libraries bring historical collections forward in space and time? How do libraries construct spaces and systems that incorporate new technologies and are open to future possibilities for engagement with library resources and services? And how do libraries create places where, amidst the convergence of past patterns and future potential, people in the present can focus attention and exercise agency to discover and create knowledge?

The Seattle Central Library that exists today, which rose into the sky above me like a transparent cathedral as I began to write this, is a design solution to questions about the past, future, and present—the temporalities—of the library. With its Book Spiral at the center, memories of the past are organized around and spread out from the core of the building. Useful technologies are present throughout the building, from automated conveyors of books and people to computers that connect the physical library to a larger information environment. And suspended in metal and glass around the Book Spiral are a variety of public areas where individuals engage with librarians, library resources and services, and each other. While not everyone is satisfied with all the aesthetic decisions that shaped the building, and more recent technological developments such as AI continue to transform it and all libraries, there are clear continuities between the historical and present functions of this exemplar library. This balance of continuity and change, adapted to different contexts, will be present in future exemplary libraries.

Since their emergence in the ancient world, three characteristics have defined libraries consistently throughout history and across diverse cultures. These characteristics concern culture, collection, and community. First, a library begins with an intention to configure and represent a particular culture through texts or fixed expressions of knowledge, such as records or books. Culture is a complex concept and phenomenon, but one way of defining it is identifying how a community or society answers and lives into Immanuel Kant's three ultimate questions: What can we know? What may we hope? What should we do? Second, a library is a collection created through the selection of texts judged worthy of attention. Through this process of discernment, librarians create a canonical or coherent context for discovery. Third, a library mediates access to its collection through a variety of information systems, spaces, and services. This is done for a specific community, whose members actively shape the culture that is shaping them and the library. From the earliest libraries in ancient Sumerian cities to modern libraries in cities like Seattle, these three principal actions—of intention, selection, and mediation—are the consistent markers of what a great library has been, is, and will continue to be.

The Seattle Public Library is one of the busiest library systems in the United Stated. In addition to its central library, SPL has twenty-six branch libraries located throughout the city—each scaled in resources, services, and spaces and adapted for its unique neighborhood. There is a route from the neighborhood pub to my house in Seattle that, at the midpoint, passes by one of these libraries. On some evenings, when inspiration for a project is unfocused or confused, I will choose this path and wander into the library to browse books selected by local librarians. Depending on my mood, I might look for something historical, something fictional, or something practical; and I almost always find something interesting. If not, I wander into the stacks and browse the beginning of the Dewey Decimal Classification scheme—the 000s, where one may find books, in various genres, related to knowledge, libraries, and computers. On a good day I will select a few books, find a comfortable seat, and begin to enhance my memory, imagination, or reason. Sometimes I find an answer to a question I had or did not realize I had. Other times I imagine new questions, seek guidance from the reference librarian, and discover additional resources in the building or, more often, online. And usually, by discovering an alternative or augmented idea, I find a new way of being in the world.

That experience of discovery, both serendipitous and sought, is what a good library enables. A library is a place designed intentionally for the discovery of resources and services that will fulfill some informational goal or hope. It is a unique place with a distinctive purpose, focused on neither a particular product like a publisher nor a purchase like a bookstore. And it is scaled for humans and their own self-selected goals, unlike the commercialized internet or a social networking site dependent on advertising revenue. Whereas many information providers exist to sell us goods and services—or collect and sell our personal data—libraries exist to open up a world of possibilities beyond the simple economics of exchange. They are about human purpose, not corporate profits. Presuming there will be a future inhabited by humans, libraries empower actions for participating in desirable futures. This engages hope, which is more than an optimistic feeling about the future but rather a reasoned approach to it that is essential for human agency. Bringing goals to the library, ranging from the mundane to the magnificent, we may hope information will be found and that our use of it will lead to some outcome—that the library will function as a portal to a future shaped by that desired outcome. Inscribed over the portal of every library should be the words, "Attend to all hope, you who enter here."

A number of years ago, I taught a first-year university seminar on the future of the book. While preparing for the course, I was also preparing a future scenarios exercise for my staff and writing a library history paper. My class evolved into a course about the future of the library, and at the end—because I had talked about it so much—my students asked for a visit to the Seattle Central Library. At the edge of the Reading Room on the top public floor, with collections and patrons spread out below, we discussed how Jorge Luis Borges's short story "The Library of Babel," about an antilibrary that contains every possible book—including books without words and books of false texts—was more like the internet than a library. Intention, selection, and mediation are absent in the Library of Babel, so its inhabitants live lives not only without true books but also without meaning or purpose. Unable to live without hopes for these, they desperately seek them; but their desires for fulfillment remain unrealized. When people challenge the value or relevance of libraries, I imagine libraries such as SPL receding into the Antilibrary of Babel in which meaning, purpose, and hope are lost. As our information environment continues to grow in complexity and Babelesque qualities, exacerbated with problematic content generated and disseminated by AI, libraries remain important institutions for shaping this environment and our participation in it. As AI continues to advance, and it becomes more challenging to distinguish real hopes for AI amidst so much false hype, libraries and librarians can help discern how human agency may best interact with new forms of artificial agency. They will do this by enabling us collectively to remember what is helpful from the past, to anticipate desirable futures, and to engage the present with hope.

2 PANDEMIC

In 2014, Emily St. John Mandel published *Station Eleven*, a novel about a flu pandemic that kills most of the world's population. For a few survivors, survival is insufficient, and they begin to reestablish markers of human civilization. One of the main characters curates a museum of civilization at an airport. The museum is a collection of objects that no longer have any practical use, but which people want to preserve, such as computers, engines, and passports. Fifteen years after the pandemic, the curator is handed three sheets of rough paper by a traveling trader. The sheets are three issues of a newspaper, published by a librarian, and include news of current events as well as content from a library: an Emily Dickinson poem and an excerpt from a biography of Abraham Lincoln. As the curator reflects on this new artifact, he wonders "what else might be possible?" It signifies, he imagines, the dawning of a new day.

In 2022, Mandel published the novel *Sea of Tranquility*, which includes more pandemics. One of these, the COVID-19 novel coronavirus, is now part of our history. Another pandemic occurs in the book's future, while the fictional author Olive Llewelyn is on a book tour for her own pandemic novel. Mandel, drawing from her own experiences writing about and living through a pandemic, imagines Llewelyn lecturing during a lockdown on the popularity of postapocalyptic literature in Llewelyn's time. "[W]e have a desire to believe that we're living at the climax of the story," she speculates. "We want to believe that we're uniquely important, that we're living at the end of history." Llewelyn pauses and observes a note she made about George Vancouver. Standing on the deck of his ship, the *HMS Discovery*, Vancouver anxiously gazed at a landscape that had been largely depopulated by plagues in the eighteenth century. That land would later bear his name, and his observations would serve as a record of an Indigenous apocalypse. Llewelyn continues, "it always *is* the end of the world"—which is "a continuous and never-ending process." But there are times when interest in postapocalyptic fiction increases, Llewelyn acknowledges, and she connects this with a fear of technological change. Our present is such a time, which has made Mandel's novels bestsellers.

Libraries figure prominently in postapocalyptic literature as signs of hope. Sometimes, the audacity of this hope inspires rage. In Cormac McCarthy's postapocalyptic novel *The Road* (2006), the unnamed father in the book stands in the ruins of a library, among shelves toppled and paper burnt to negate the value of books "predicated on a world to come" in a space that "was itself an expectation." More often, though, libraries are preserved as a redemptive technology, or re-created as a transformative technology. However anxious we may be about new and powerful technologies—ships of conquest, weapons of mass destruction, industrial disasters, superintelligent machines—we continue to develop libraries as enduring systems for creating a better future. This hope is not merely an optimistic expectation that libraries can improve things in the future. Hope in libraries is grounded in past and present experiences of them doing so, and trust that that they will continue to do so.

Most of us, in history and around the world today, first encountered the library through physical collections and people behind desks. These remain common experiences, but for more than fifty years information and communication technologies have added a new digital dimension to the library. In early 2020, when much of the world went into lockdown in an effort to slow the spread of COVID-19, we became aware of our dependencies on both digital *and* embodied forms of engagement. For libraries, the lockdown revealed the robustness of the digital dimension of today's libraries. This was not a new revelation—libraries have been augmenting resources and services digitally for decades—but the pandemic demonstrated the extent to which continuity of operations could be sustained largely through digital technologies.

On one hand, this was a moment of great success for libraries. Decades of automating operations, networking computers, facilitating access to electronic resources, and providing digital services enabled libraries to continue to function online and even develop newer services, such as contactless pickup and virtual events. On the other hand, this was a moment of great loss for librarians. Libraries are situated locally in communities and presume the presence of people in buildings: browsing and reading physical materials, having face-to-face conversations and meetings, and sitting in chairs and working at desks. Technology access has been a priority for libraries for many years also, but this has been dependent on in-person services, physical computers, and wireless networks in buildings. (Some of these networks remained accessible in parking lots outside of library buildings during the pandemic, even if the computers inside were not.) As much as the digital dimension of the library has expanded in recent decades, library buildings staffed with librarians have remained a primary and privileged interface for libraries. Even today, when people speak of "the library," they often mean a building—not the much more complex infrastructure of which a library's building is part. Our blended online-offline experiences during the COVID-19 pandemic, which included positive interactions as well as negative isolation and too much private suffering, complicated a simple, dualistic view of our technologically entangled world. For librarians, it revealed that a library includes and must be designed for both embodied and digital engagements that center human needs and limitations.

At the 1962 Seattle World's Fair—which was called the Century 21 Exposition and, in the words of local historians Paula Becker and Alan Stein, presented "a future ginned up from science-fiction mystique mixed with cutting edge science"—the American Library Association created a "Library 21" exhibit to show how libraries were integrating "machines into an environment of books." This "Library of the Future" exhibit included a UNIVAC (a universal automatic computer), microformats, fax machines, and other electronic devices alongside more traditional reference, adult, and children's books as well as reference and readers' advisory services. Although the demonstrated use of the UNIVAC to provide bibliographic and other factual information did not become common in libraries, its presence signified that a new technological transformation of libraries, including automation, was underway. The pandemic affirmed a digital trajectory that at least three generations of librarians have been pursuing, but the nearly all-digital work of pandemic librarianship revealed dimensions of the library that cannot or should not be automated or mediated digitally. In a way, with only one form of connection—remote and distanced, and often asynchronous—the pandemic provided us with a glimpse of a dystopian future of constrained hopes. As libraries continue to explore and implement more algorithmically mediated forms of access, they will need to attend to the relationship between automation and alienation. More automation, enabled by new forms of AI, could lead to more isolation and related privations. Pandemic librarianship also revealed how transformative technologies can be sources of hope instead of fear, as they are able to help us shape new and better futures. Libraries' long and continuing productive integration of new and emerging technologies into human-centered and human-scaled systems are a model for other institutions that seek to enable human agency while respecting human limits and diverse needs.

3 BECOMING A LIBRARIAN

At the age of sixteen, Umberto Eco wandered into a dark library in a medieval Benedictine monastery in the Province of Rome. There, open on a lectern, he found the *Acta Sanctorum* in which he could read about incredible acts attributed to his namesake St. Umberto. Some thirty years later, the impression of that experience resulted in a setting for a medieval detective story: a massive but secret labyrinthine library. About the time Eco began working on this first novel of his, published in 1980 with the enigmatic title *The Name of the Rose*, I was encountering a much more mundane manifestation of the library. Growing up in the final quarter of the twentieth century, in a developing suburb of a modern city struggling with social and technological changes, a public library was a common, even expected, part of the local social infrastructure.

The building to which my mother drove me regularly was a mid-modern box, with an aesthetic more brutal than beckoning. The center of the building was filled with new media including audio, video, and micro formats. Tall ranges of books created alcoves at the periphery. The building was barely a decade old, but it was cramped and full of library materials as well as retired and unemployed people passing time under harsh lighting and on uncomfortable furniture. (When my father joined the growing number of unemployed people in the region, I learned that the library also had resources for studying and starting businesses.) At first, I was deposited in the children's area, where I could browse and peruse fantasy and mystery books and escape the predictable world for a while. Occasionally, a librarian would show an entertaining reel-to-reel film in a community room. When I became bored with the materials classified for my age, I began wandering into the book alcoves. The more substantial books I discovered there revealed a world much larger and more complex than the small and homogenous world in which I was being raised. My suburban library's modest collection was not awe-inspiring, but the material presence of so much accumulated knowledge—and of the human keepers of this trust—opened up my imagination to new possibilities and alternative worlds. As Rita Dove said of the public library of her youth, "All the time in the world was there, and sometimes / all the world on a single page." A modest public library, like Eco's monastic library, is a revealer of complexity and mystery.

By the time I was able to drive myself to it, I knew my local public library was, as the nineteenth-century founders of such institutions had intended, a "great engine" of education and exploration. As I spent more time in public, school, and academic libraries, I became more aware and appreciative of the human and technological infrastructure necessary to facilitate access to a deep and extensive range of human understanding and experience. When the internet became part of the library—providing remote access first to the catalog, then to electronic resources—the reach of the library extended into a whole new environment. In graduate school, I began working in archives full of carefully curated manuscript pages and early imprints. Exploring those ancient sources of and structures for knowledge, I began to appreciate the historical depth and global reach of the library as an institution. Eventually, this growing awareness culminated in a sense of vocation.

One day, while studying an apocalyptic Dead Sea Scroll text for a doctoral seminar, I paused to contemplate a gloss written nearly two thousand years ago: "God told Habakkuk to write down the things that are going to come upon the last generation." I reflected on the fact that this text, created by a group that had withdrawn into the wilderness to await the final coming of God, was part of a library. Suddenly I realized that this scroll library, established to interpret the history and future of the world through one community's experiences, was an emblem of every library. This revelation was a personal apocalypse—of the good sort. A series of past and prospective moments—connected with my experiences of libraries in life and literature—converged and cohered: I was a child, seeking unknown books in cold metal stacks; I was an undergraduate, overwhelmed by the inviolable intellectual and physical structures imposed on knowledge and space; I was a young adult, inspired by the glorious myths of the ancient Library of Alexandria and intrigued by the failure of hope in the fictional Library of Babel; I was a graduate student, rapturous over unending discoveries in great research libraries; I was a researcher, perplexed by hidden collections, online resources, and offsite storage facilities; I was an editorial assistant, working with digital images and encoding software to create a critical edition of an apocalyptic text. In that moment, seated in a library that had had a role in recovering the texts of the Dead Sea Scroll library, I glimpsed something of the past and future of the institution called the library. I realized that I wanted to be part of the collaborative generational effort to curate and cultivate it, to sustain its revelatory power from being lost in the wilderness or online, and to seek the vision of Alexandria over against the specter of Babel.

Robert Logan and Marshall McLuhan described the library of my youth as "an old figure in a new ground." As new audial and visual media entered mainstream library collections, and as librarians began to help people duplicate and reassemble information with photocopiers and computers, the role of the library was shifting from a more "passive distributor of the information artifacts of others to that of the manufacturer of information on par with a publisher, a filmmaker, or a broadcaster." Writing about the future of the library in the 1970s, Logan and McLuhan claimed, "We are moving into an age in which information is becoming the prime concern of mankind, the key to survival in a complicated environment." Today—on the other side of the advent of the internet and the internet of things, social media and big data, mobile and cloud computing, and automated and autonomous technologies—their charge to libraries in the electronic and multimedia information age resonates a generation later in our digital and AI information age: "The challenge facing libraries is to fully exploit the new technologies while at the same time preserving the best of the past traditions of the library."

When I entered library school at the beginning of the twenty-first century, we focused on how digital and globally networked resources and services were adding a new dimension to the library. My career since has involved integrating digital technologies into every aspect of library work: what and how we collect, how we facilitate human and technological access to and use of information resources, and how we design both physical and virtual places for engagement with information. Within the last few years, libraries have been exploring how new forms of AI, such as generative AI, will further transform the discovery, creation, and use of information. The scope and scale of digital transformation has highlighted the role of the library as an agent of social as well as technological transformation. During the COVID-19 pandemic, it was necessary to pursue digital-first strategies, which accelerated not only the digital transformation of libraries but the realization that libraries and their communities are becoming "postdigital." This means that digital technologies are no longer novel or supplemental, but embedded in and entangled with current social and technological practices. Recent advances in AI have further accelerated the integration of the digital into our lives and world. The challenge and hope now—for libraries, but also for the communities and cultures they sustain—is to ensure that the "new ground," constituted by new and emerging technologies, is integrated wisely into the "old figure" of the library.

4 WHY LIBRARIES?

When certain people discover I am a library director—say a software engineer, a car salesman, or a university trustee (just to pick a few interactions I have had while writing this book)—I anticipate certain questions. Isn't everything online? Do you still use card catalogs and/or the Dewey Decimal System? Do we *really* still need libraries these days? I used to respond to such questions quickly, and not always charitably, with ready answers: libraries spend significant amounts of money to provide access to content that is not on the open internet; librarians help people find the best information and use it well; libraries provide unique spaces that enable people to participate in the discovery, creation, and sharing of knowledge. Others I meet—such as aeronautical engineers, high-school teachers, and architects (again, just to pick a few other recent interactions)—have a different set of questions. How will libraries ensure long-term access to digital records? How are librarians helping people access and use digital books and AI research tools? How are virtual and augmented reality technologies changing library spaces? My initial responses to these types of questions typically focused on something about which I thought the questioner was ignorant: *collecting* to preserve digital materials; *digital* and AI as part of information literacy and ethics; the *blending* of digital and physical environments and experiences.

But as I grew tired of my prepared elevator speeches, and a bit wiser about people's hopes and desires, I started to wonder more about the past experiences of each person asking me about the future of libraries. Seeking to learn what they thought libraries are for, I began responding with my own questions: When was the last time you used a library, and what did you use it for? How do you find and access information for your work and life? Whom do you trust to help you discover, select, validate, and use information? What resources and services are the libraries near you offering? Whatever I say next is a response to—and an attempt to update or deepen—a particular person's image and expectations of the library. Not all institutions age well, but the library has proven itself to be not just relevant but crucial for millennia. It is also one of the few highly trusted and valued institutions in our society. As we navigate the significant social and technological transformations that characterizes our present moment—especially in connection with AI—we are experiencing an extreme "elevation of information" as a prime concern for thriving in our complex information environment. What we know, how we know what we know, and how we respond to what we know are fundamental questions each of us faces daily.

Information has always been central to human existence: we seek it to survive as well as thrive—to eat, to mate, to learn, to create, to understand ourselves and our place in the universe. With the creation of information artifacts some five millennia ago, information became more materially fixed and thus more reliably transferable across time and spaces, which extended its life, role, and power. Libraries were created to provide immediate and long-term access to material information artifacts, and this remains a core function of libraries today. Over the last fifty years, though, we have seen "an information turn." New information and communication technologies have been significantly reshaping our lives and the environments in which we live. Luciano Floridi says that, especially now, questions concerning the "creation, dynamics, management, and utilization of information and computational resources are absolutely vital." Today's information and communication technologies have ancient ancestors, but their present pervasiveness, portability, and power is unprecedented. Tomorrow's technologies will be even greater—processing, discovering, and creating information we never could have on our own.

For those who see only our new and emerging technological environment, many wonder about the future of the ancient figure of the library. Does the internet, as a new infrastructure for—as well as an image of—information access, render the old institution of the library irrelevant? Will artificial agents replace human mediators of information? Like other innovative information and communication technologies before it, the internet has certainly and significantly changed libraries and how people use them. Digital and globally networked resources and services are now part of nearly every library's infrastructure, and these have changed the physical places to which these are linked. AI will change libraries significantly as well, further altering the ways we engage with information and blend human and technological mediations to leverage the distinctive capabilities of each. While enduring images of the library's antiquity and physicality distinguish it from the more abstract and ethereal images of the internet and disembodied AI, there are more fundamental distinctions between the library and these technologies. The internet, which is more open and less mediated by humans, suggests the promise of all information for anything. But the library remains an intentionally developed and socially mediated institution, providing access to better information and enabling people to use it well. In addition to information access, a library is concerned with empowering people to decide what information is worthy of their attention and how they will exercise their agency with regard to it. AI systems can help us discover and create new information, both in collaboration with us and independent of us, but these need to be designed to advance—and their autonomy should be governed by—human values and goals.

Klaus Schwab of the World Economic Forum claims that transformative digital technologies such as big data (i.e., the analysis of large datasets), cloud computing, and AI have created a "fourth industrial revolution" that is "fundamentally changing the way we live, work, and relate to one another." More profoundly, Floridi argues we are living through a fourth modern scientific revolution, an "information revolution," in which our dependence on automated information processing by artificial agents is "affecting our sense of self, how we relate to each other, and how we shape and interact with our world." This revolution is revealing the importance of information in shaping us and our world, and it casts "new light on who we are and how we are related to the world." Throughout history, information and communication technologies have changed both how we interpret and how we design the world. Now, Floridi points out, "Smart and autonomous agents no longer need to be human," and we are shaping a world that is increasingly "friendly" to artificial agents. Information, and its relationship to the formation of our individual and collective attention and agency, is now one of our age's prime concerns.

Within the last ten years, especially following the introduction of popular digital assistants such as Amazon's Alexa, AI has become a ubiquitous and general-purpose technology like the steam engine, electricity, and the digital computer. Very recently, we have witnessed the sophistication with which generative AI can create new information through texts, images, music, code, and more. (Although too much of what AI generates currently is only pseudo information, something that is fake or false.) AI is now a regular part of our daily lives and our social imagination, rapidly transforming what we do, how we understand ourselves and our world, and what we will become and do. The increasing role and power of artificial agents in our lives raises a number of questions about how all the data collected by and for these applications are obtained and used, about the influences the algorithms that drive these systems have on our actions, and about the broader social and environmental impacts of complex autonomous systems operating without sufficient human responsibility and accountability. The significance and scale of the technological challenges and opportunities facing us require us to understand and proactively shape an information environment that ensures automated intelligence augments rather than inhibits human intelligence, hopes, and agency. The library—which has a proven history of curating and cultivating information artifacts, access, and agency—has a unique role and responsibility as intelligent technologies advance. By designing new automated information processes as well as new human information practices, libraries can help shape a good information environment for both natural and artificial information agents—an environment that is aligned with and advances human values and the hopes they inspire.

PART TWO

THE LIBRARY AS AN ARCHIVE: HOW LIBRARIES ARE SOURCES OF HOPE

B   Philosophy, Psychology, Religion
C–F   History
G   Geography, Anthropology

5 THE EMERGENCE OF ATTENTION AND IMAGINATION

One of the distinctives of our species is our ability to imagine alternative realities. The earliest forms of life evolved as reflexive information processing agents, collecting environmental data through natural sensors and then reacting to survive. But *Homo sapiens*, emerging between two hundred thousand and fifty thousand years ago, became dis-automatized from this instinctive information-seeking drive and began to reflect on the meaning of information. Information precedes and exists independently of us, but *Homo sapiens* crossed a semantic threshold by thinking about information abstractly and imaginatively instead of reflexively and automatically. In *Sapiens: A Brief History of Humankind*, Yuval Harari calls this moment in human evolutionary history the "Tree of Knowledge mutation." Harari's allusion to the Garden of Eden, and the story of humans' expulsion from it, signifies the moral significance of this turning point in human evolution and development.

A suite of traits associated with reflective attention—enhanced working memory, abstract reasoning, conceptual self-awareness, symbolic thinking, grammatical language, and instruction—made possible the creation of symbolic mental worlds. This enabled humans to explore, transcend, and change reality by imagining alternatives to actual past and present experiences, as well as anticipated futures. Humans were able also to comprehend and communicate information as well as pseudo information—false "disinformation" and misleading "misinformation"—about observed phenomena, the minds of others, unobserved phenomena, and future possibilities. Collectively, they were able to develop innovative plans, meaningful stories, social systems, and new environments. Through reflective attention, humans became open to new understandings of themselves and the world. Their desires and hopes broadened, and they extended themselves beyond their initial present conditions.

The emergence of reflective attention and imagination could be called the first human information revolution. Archeological evidence of it is found in the artifacts created during the technological revolution that accompanied the emergence of our species—an explosion of technologies for personal ornamentation, art, elaborate burials, complex multicomponent weaponry, long-distance trade, timekeeping, and scheduling. Before then, about three million years ago, early hominins had begun developing stone tools and related techniques to improve their diets. Over time, as lithic and other technologies became more sophisticated, human biology began to change and become more dependent on technology. Mental and motor skills capable of purposely manipulating raw materials and transforming them into reusable tools evolved, and humans came to rely on fire for digestible food, clothing in the absence of fur, and shelters for habitations. Merging with natural selection, human technological development codirected evolution and eventually outpaced it. From the beginning, technology has been entangled with human agency.

The ability to develop aspirational desires and goals over more basic drives and demands is not easily maintained. As Adam Gazzaley and Larry Rosen explain in *The Distracted Mind: Ancient Brains in a High-Tech World*, "the very essence of what has evolved furthest in our brains to make us human—our ability to set high-level goals for ourselves—collides headfirst with our brains' fundamental limitations in cognitive control: attention, working memory, and goal management." This imbalance between aspirational goals and cognitive limits, they conclude, remains "a fundamental vulnerability." To leverage information attention, humans needed—and still need—to develop social and technological structures to sustain and augment our attention and agency collectively.

A fundamental challenge we face today with our current information revolution, related to automation, is the extent to which it threatens the dis-automatization connected with the origin of our species that resulted in our capacity for reflective attention. "Attention merchants," with the help of AI, compete for, capture, and commoditize our attention in ways that interfere with our ability to focus and do what we want to do. James Williams argues that this type of functional distraction can lead to an existential form of distraction, if our higher goals and values are compromised and we are hindered from being who we desire to be over time. These forms of distraction can lead to an even deeper, epistemic form. This form of distraction diminishes fundamental capacities—such as reflection, imagination, reasoning, and metacognition—which enable us to define our values and hopes in the first place.

If intelligence can be said to exist in nonhuman animals and complex information-processing technologies, what distinguishes human intelligence may be found in our distinctive aspirations. Simone Weil claimed that "intelligence can only be led by desire ... intelligence grows and bears fruit in joy." Desire, joy, and hope are rooted in attention. This is not an individual concern exclusively: in one of her last notebooks, Weil asked, "What is culture?," and answered, "formation of attention." Between the information revolution associated with attention, which gave us new capabilities for reflective attention and imagination, and the information revolution related to the automated processing of information, which is producing automated forms of intelligence with very different attention mechanisms, two other information revolutions produced innovations that can help us manage both human and artificial attention: information agencies, such as libraries, and information artifacts, such as books. These enduring human innovations enable us to extend collective knowledge and shared hopes into the future—as well as to create new futures.

6 LIVING LIBRARIES

Books are a relatively recent carrier of culture. Long before there were books or other information artifacts, cultural narratives and traditions were shared by living people. Although some spoken texts were parts of more complex cycles and epics, oral texts were often short and attention spans—cultivated to remember, hear, and retell—were, it seems, longer than they are now. Before writing, cultures created impressive artifacts that communicated what was possible with them; but these cultures were sustained and transmitted primarily through spoken memories, understandings, and instruction. Artifacts that outlive their interpretive communities, however, communicate little. The most ancient stories and sayings to which we have access, represented in the earliest writings as well as through enduring oral traditions, are about explorations and explanations of origins and genealogies, changes and transformations, cultural values and practices, and the place and purpose of humans in the world.

After the creation of the book, nature came to be seen as a kind of book—it was the first book of the creator to be read alongside the books created by humans. It is, of course, more accurate to say that the book is a creation than to say that creation is a book. Ancient cultures remind us that creation, shaped by an agency that preceded us and is greater than us, remains our first teacher. But our creations can cause us to miss what the book of creation reveals. We understand our own creations better and often prioritize the products of our own agency, mistaking the partial representation for the fuller reality. A similar narrowing of perspective happened with the shift from oral to written literacy. Plato famously records Socrates' concerns about preserving the benefits of oral literacy—memory, questioning, dialogue, and collaborative learning—as reliance on written texts was becoming more common. Ironically, we remember and know about Socrates' concerns about reading and writing technologies through Plato's books. But the caution about our information artifacts, from books to AI, closing us off from other sources of information remains important.

In Christianity, the doctrine of the incarnation holds that the eternal Word become flesh to dwell among humans to reveal a new life of love. The incarnate word was not just a living book but a living apocalypse, revealing a divine message about transcendent wisdom, a promised future, and how the world was being made right in the present. The Christian message about this new "book" of creation was first transmitted orally, and then also inscribed in various genres—testimonies, chronicles, letters, apocalypses. Even though the written witness became central for Christians and the textual cultures influenced by them, oral and lived witnesses remained important and shaped traditions and communal practices. Paul wrote letters to early Christians telling them that they were living epistles and warning that "the letter kills but the Spirit gives life" (2 Corinthians 3:6). Too often, however, the killing letter has been prioritized over the life-giving spirit. In libraries, though, there is hope that some dead letters may find new life. Frederick Buechner says that when words treasured in a library "move us closer to that truth and gentleness of spirit by which we become fully human ... the Word itself becomes flesh again and again and dwells among us and within us, full of grace and truth."

The oral legends and histories preserved by Indigenous Coast Salish peoples of the Pacific Northwest emphasize creation as the primary source of revelation. "Learning from the land" is one way of describing these cultures. The stories told in such cultures concern much more than the preservation and transmission of information: they cultivate sensibilities and skills so that each person may attend to vocational and moral guidance revealed through creation. According to Jill La Pointe, "Understanding our place and role in creation was shaped through our ability to listen and learn from creation in all its forms." National forms of colonialism attempted to force the primacy of the written word on the Indigenous people of the Northwest through treaties and land claims. But communication and information technologies also provided "different canoes" for transmitting Indigenous wisdom, histories, and stories. We are able to read and learn from these stories now because they were collected from members of a living library, recorded on tapes, translated and transcribed into written texts, stored on computers, and printed in books. Archived in libraries, these stories will continue to find new life in future readers.

Libraries are created by those who have what the seventeenth-century English scholar Samuel Purchas called the "literall advantage"—the power of reading and writing. This creates an immense asymmetry in the historical record, since not all communications are able to be reduced to writing and inscribed on durable media. Many voices are underrepresented or not represented at all. Some were missed, some were ignored, and some were excluded or even erased. Moreover, most communications throughout human history have not been recorded, especially when we consider "prehistory"—the term used since the mid nineteenth century to refer to history before the written record. The texts that have survived were created in particular contexts, the product of conversations in both private and public spaces, and we often know little about how texts fit within broader dialogues and textual cultures. Those voices to which we have access now exist through a combination of intentional collection, benign neglect, broad use, and random accidents.

Libraries—individually and in aggregate—are incomplete. They are only one way of accessing the imagination and actions of the living and the dead. Even in the present, with the automatic capture and creation of so much digital information, little of this is likely to survive into the far future as useful or even usable information. Digital materials depend on assemblages of software and hardware that age into obsolescence, planned or unplanned, and break when abandoned. And little of our digital culture is being curated actively by memory institutions such as libraries. There was life before the library and there is life beyond the library, but libraries are now a necessary part of our lives and we depend on them to sustain human cultures and hopes. AI is not only a new cultural artifact but a new type of cultural artifact that libraries can use to recover, discover, include, preserve, and increase the diversity of human cultures.

7 THE CITY

About twelve thousand years ago, some humans began to manipulate the lives of a select number of animals and plants to provide supplies of food, raw materials, and muscle power. Clearing forests and fields, digging canals and ploughing furrows, building houses and walls, these humans became adept at creating artificial environments within natural ones. In some cases, these increasingly complex environments, which required sophisticated social systems for organizing rules, trade, and cultural activities, resulted in one of the most significant technological innovations of our species: cities.

The earliest cities were organized many millennia ago, independently, in Asia and Europe, in Africa, and in both Americas. Around the planet, local consensus recurrently emerged about the value of living in cities and they became a distinct feature of human development. Cities comprised a set of technologies that provided some stability, security, economies of scale, new opportunities for specialization, and the creation of cultural goods. At the same time, cities created new social hierarchies and inequalities, food insecurity and disease, and more impersonal relationships. And, often with devastating effects, they permanently altered physical environments. Nevertheless, for millennia cities have been a central part of the human experience and one of our favored environmental niches.

To realize complex, shared, and future-oriented goals—to leverage the benefits of collective intelligence—cities organized a variety of information agencies. Following the first information revolution associated with information attention, this second information revolution involved the creation of political, economic, religious, and other institutions to aggregate human attention and agency and create new structures for shared agency. These information agencies organized laws for courts, accounting for markets, narratives for temples, and other social arrangements for other collaborative processes that supported, structured, and sustained civic life. These cultural institutions created new forms of structural agency that enabled cities to operate as multi-agent and semi-autonomous systems to extend collective human actions across space and time.

In history and the imagination, cities are often viewed as ambiguous places. The city is a technological site of ingenuity but also of iniquity, of innovation and injustice, of prosperity and inequity, of inspiration and desperation. Ambivalence about the city is evident in the ancient story of Babel. A group of migrants comes together to build a city, make a name for itself, and avoid being scattered. The imagined city promises a place where, together, people may be freed from migratory challenges—of securing food, shelter, and safety—and enjoy thriving in a more permanent place instead of surviving in a more precarious one. But, as their city's tower rises into the heavens, God, impressed with their technological accomplishment, confuses the one people's language and disrupts their shared hopes and agency. This halts their creative work, and their fears of being scattered are realized. According to Walter Brueggemann, the judgment against Babel is against a self-serving autonomy that "seeks to survive by its own resources." Alluding to the seat of the ancient Babylonian Empire, the story of Babel can be read more specifically as a critique of imperial or oppressive forms of autonomy—of the creation of independent systems and structures for autonomous agency that become in- and anti-human. Human hopes, the story of Babel suggests, are not inherently or necessarily good.

As we consider the impact of new complex technologies associated with our current information revolution, Brett Frischmann and Evan Selinger worry we are losing our agency and downgrading ourselves as we develop artificial autonomous systems. "What meaningfully distinguishes *Homo sapiens* from all other species is our capability to imagine, conceptualize, and engineer ourselves and our environment," they argue. Our humanity "is reflected in us and our built world of imagined realities, institutions, infrastructures, and environments." We need to be attentive to how our identities, societies, and world can be controlled, conditioned, and constrained by our own creations. The structural forms of automated and autonomous agency we are capable of creating, from cities to AI, become oppressive and require regular human interventions to correct systemic flaws and failures. Those flaws and failures flow from our hopes, both good and bad, which are always limited and require constant critical reflection, reimagination, refinement, and enlargement.

Frank Pasquale argues we have the means to "channel" technologies of automation and not be "captured" by them. The best performing AI applications are often those designed to complement human agents. If we focus on collaborative relationships with AI that are complementary rather than competitive, we may realize further technological advancements that could bring "better health care, education, and more to all of us, while maintaining meaningful work." Focusing on how AI may complement human agency, Pasquale replaces Isaac Asimov's famous laws of robots with four new ones for AI. AI systems should (1) complement and not replace professionals, (2) not counterfeit humanity, (3) not intensify zero-sum races for resources, and (4) identify their creators, controllers, and owners. One of the information agencies created in ancient cities—which remains a vital information interface and infrastructure in most cities today—is the library. The library in Babel or Babylon would have been constrained with serving imperial ends, but today most librarians serve the public. Public-serving libraries, as social infrastructures for the common good, are well positioned to enhance human agency within an increasingly automated environment. As Shannon Mattern argues, libraries have critical roles helping people understand and engage with our information environment. They can serve "simultaneously as an epistemological scaffolding, access provider, infrastructure manager, privacy trainer, zone of digital security, champion of open-access materials and sustainable public-interest technologies, and space of social connection and inclusions." To imagine how AI might impact the future of research and our knowledge ecosystem, in 2024 the Association of Research Libraries and the Coalition for Networked Information developed four plausible but divergent future scenarios. The most desirable and hopeful scenario imagines AI augmenting human agency rather than it becoming inhibited or eclipsed by commercial interests or autonomous agency. In this scenario, in which libraries and librarians have a central role, social intentionality and responsiblility in the design and adaptation of AI creates a world in which human and computational capabilities are integrated and flourish.

8 THE BEGINNING OF THE BOOK

The Epic of Gilgamesh is a series of stories about an ancient king's search for fame and immortality. In what has become a standard organization of this narrative, there is a statement about why this text came to exist in material form:

> [Gilgamesh] saw what was secret and revealed what was hidden,
> He brought back tidings from before the flood,
> From a distant journey came home, weary, at peace,
> Engraved all his hardships on a monument of stone ...

After many adventures, Gilgamesh eventually realizes he cannot avoid his return to clay. But in the end, through writing, his dream of immortality is realized: his tale becomes a text inscribed on a stone monument and, later, on clay tablets that moved through space and time and entered the collections of libraries.

The textual immortality of Gilgamesh, preserved on tablets carried over many miles and centuries, was suspended for more than two millennia. In 1853, while excavating the ancient city of Nineveh, the archaeologist Hormund Rassam uncovered the palace and library of a long-forgotten Assyrian king, Ashurbanipal. A scribe as well as a king, Ashurbanipal built what may have been one of the greatest library collections of the ancient world for the practical management and literary prestige of his kingdom. Soon after his death, however, in 612 BCE Nineveh was destroyed and depopulated. Among the ruins of Ashurbanipal's library, Ransom and others found some twenty-eight thousand cuneiform clay tablets. David Damrosch claims the discovery comprised "one of the greatest collections of literature ever recovered from the ancient world." This collection consisted of administrative archival records as well as historical, religious, scientific, and literary works—including numerous copies of the epic stories of Gilgamesh.

FIGURE 8.1 The Library of Ashurbanipal on Display in the British Museum, used with permission

In the early nineteenth century, the founding professor and librarian of Princeton Theological Seminary, Archibald Alexander, shared with his students what was at that time the received wisdom about the origin of writing:

> at an early period in the history of the world it appeared good to infinite wisdom to direct that the revelations which were made to man should be committed to writing. As there is no evidence of any more ancient writings than those of Moses, it is reasonable to conclude that the making of books originated in divine appointment and was performed by divine assistance.

Alexander admitted that the "history of the origin of alphabetical writing is involved in considerable obscurity." According to his knowledge—and his knowledge was extensive for the time—the first record of a written record appeared in the book of Exodus, when Moses is commanded to create a record of a people that would not be remembered. Soon after that, "the law was written by the finger of JEHOVAH, on the two tables of testimony." Therefore, Alexander concluded, "this wonderful art [of writing], so necessary for recording the revelations received from God, for the use of posterity" was "no invention of man, but a revelation from God."

Later in the nineteenth century, the archeological discoveries of Nineveh and other lost cities of the Ancient Near East extended the history of the world and writing. The amount of past time that had been kept, lost, and rediscovered to be kept again reached back to include city-states that emerged in the fourth millennium BCE in southern Mesopotamia. As methods of cultivation and commerce advanced within the farming communities that had settled around the Tigris and Euphrates rivers, the complexities of urban existence required rules and records. By the third millennium BCE, in Gilgamesh's Uruk and in other nearby cities, mnemonic pictographic symbols had evolved into a coded system of wedge-shaped marks called cuneiform—the earliest known form of writing. Administrative and literary texts were inscribed on stone and clay tablets, initially to manage the present affairs of cities but increasingly to reflect on a deeper past and a farther future.

The book of Genesis, which reflects traces of stories from the Gilgamesh cycle (such as an account of a great deluge), begins with speech: the spoken word of God that creates the cosmos out of chaos. In the Garden of Eden, in the third chapter of Genesis, speech is quickly used against God by a shrewd serpent who turns God into an abstraction and convinces the first humans to eat from the forbidden tree of knowledge of good and evil. For their failure to trust God's words, they are expelled from the garden. Thereafter, the pursuit and application of knowledge requires wisdom—the ability to discern what is true and good from what is false and bad, and to distinguish between what *can* be known and *could* be done from what *may* be known and *should* be done. The story of the loss of Eden warns that human intelligence should not be absolutely autonomous, and the remainder of the book that contains this story exists to aid in the disciplined augmentation of knowledge and the discernment of wisdom.

Ancient texts such as the Epic of Gilgamesh and Genesis exist today both as literary representations and physical manifestations of the invention of writing. They record the power of oral and aural experiences to disclose what can be known, and they demonstrate how the inscription of words on a durable surface extends the reach and power of information to create new knowledge and meaning. These information artifacts significantly enhanced the augmentation of knowledge and human intelligence, and they mark the advent of a third information revolution, following those associated with reflective attention and structural agency. With the intention to communicate a substantial message through a material medium, so that it may be mediated to and connect with others across space and time, we have the genesis of one the most important information artifacts: the book. Without the three elements of a message, a medium, and mediation, it is difficult to conceive of what a book was, is, or will be. Content must be carried through a material container for a reader: "no one can read a text," Jonathan Rose points out, "until it is incarnated in the material form of a book." The history of a book depends on the histories of its copies. But these information artifacts are always situated within a network of textual activities that includes the spoken word, the creation of the written word in various media, and literate engagement with the written word heard or read. It takes a textual community to enable the creation, dissemination, reception, and survival of books and knowledge. If this process of textual production and transmission is sustained over time, it becomes cyclical and enables the creation of new books and communities. AI is already part of our textual community, helping human agents at every point in the lifecycle of books—and it has the potential to augment human intelligence further through new collaborations between human and artificial agents. Sustaining a generative lifecycle of information artifacts such as books requires information agencies such as libraries to protect it against mortal and moral threats, both old and new.

9 THE BEGINNING OF THE LIBRARY

To prevent information from being lost, and to provide immediate and long-term access to communications inscribed in records and books, information and attention management structures and systems—such as archives and libraries—joined other innovative urban institutions by the second millennium BCE. Most of the earliest records, inscribed on tablets, concerned financial and legal transactions and were created and consulted for administrative purposes. Given the recordkeeping functions of these documents, the repositories that kept them are more properly called archives. But literary texts, such as the Epic of Gilgamesh, were labeled and deposited in repositories' baskets and pigeonholes, and a broader intention to configure and transmit intellectual cultures transformed many of these archives into libraries.

Initially, libraries were the technologies of and for kingdoms and empires. To shape the temporal record of his earthly reign, the scribe-king Ashurbanipal arrogated the recordkeeping power of the Mesopotamian goddess Belet-seri and created a library. A few centuries later, Alexander the Great's successors in Egypt, the Ptolemies, imagined manifesting in a library the Aristotelian ambition to order and classify the world in order to control it. So great was their ambition that the earliest myths of the size and significance of the Alexandrian library are nearly coeval with the library itself—and these outlived the library, growing over time. Details in extent historical sources, such as the number of books in the collection, exceed what is historically plausible. And however magnificent the library may have been, its glory faded quickly. By the end of the fourth century, Paulus Orosius, a student of Augustine and collaborator on *The City of God*, claimed there was no great library in Alexandria.

Then, as now, the idea of so vast and comprehensive a collection inspires the human imagination to suspend incredulity and reach beyond reality. The enduring idea associated with the Ptolemies is of a universal library: a site where the wholeness and unity of knowledge is present in and sustained through a comprehensive collection. The Letter of Aristeas, a pseudepigraphical document (literally, a falsely attributed work) from the second century BCE, is one source that records the legend of the Alexandrian ambition. This epistle purports to report the creation of the Greek translation of the Hebrew scriptures, the Septuagint, named for the seventy-two scribes who were said to have completed their work in Alexandria in seventy-two days. According to the letter, Demetrius of Phalerum, as keeper of Ptolemy II's library, had been charged to collect, "if possible, all the books in the world." "By purchase and translation," Aristeas claims, Demetrius "brought to a successful conclusion, as far as lay in his power, the king's plan." The letter uses an improbable volume count of five hundred thousand. The Septuagint was created because Demetrius discovered that the "lawbooks of the Jews" were not among the library's papyrus scrolls. Once the Hebrew scriptures had been added to the collection of the Alexandrian library, Aristeas expects the words in the scrolls of the Septuagint will be "preserved completely and permanently in perpetuity."

The Ptolemies were creators of books as well as collectors of them. Their ambition was to make Alexandria the cultural center of the Hellenistic world of which it had only recently become part. In conjunction with their library, the Ptolemies established a place for scholarly inquiry and production called the Museum, named for the daughters of Mnemosyne, the goddess of memory. Some of the greatest minds of the time gathered there, working under the inspiration of the muses of epic and lyric poetry, sacred lyrics, song and dance, comedy and tragedy, history and astronomy. The names associated with the Museum—of those who may have used and contributed to the library—include the poet and cataloger Callimachus, the mathematician Euclid, the physicist Strato, the geographer Eratosthenes, the anatomist Herophilus, and the polymath Archimedes. Livy considered the library at Alexandria "a noble work of royal taste and royal thoughtfulness." Seneca, however, thought it was an unthoughtful extravagance—books bought "for the sake of show, not for the sake of learning." Yet, while it existed, the Alexandrian library preserved the transmission of oral cultures that preceded and paralleled it, developed a physical and procedural infrastructure to organize the cultural record of the known world, and enabled the discovery and generation of new knowledge.

Linked with the legitimization of the Ptolemaic dynasty, the Alexandrian library like Ashurbanipal's fell into oblivion as its benefactors' time was superseded by others' times. But unlike Ashurbanipal's library, the power of a greater idea provisionally realized in the Alexandrian library survived: the idea of an immense collection of knowledge, or a total library, which generates even more knowledge. Such an ambition deserves epic stories of origins and ends, and such tales have enabled the Alexandrian ideal, at least, to conquer time—Aristotle's destroyer of things and memory. This ideal seeks to preserve at scale memories of past times, enable the production of knowledge in present times, and care for the media that may transfer that knowledge to future times. It is an ideal that is still invoked today, even though it now includes digital and distributed strategies.

Ancient libraries provided models and methods for bringing together the values of reflective attention, structural agency, and intelligence augmentation from the information revolutions associated with information attention, agencies, and artifacts. Over a long period of time, these values have become increasingly diverse, inclusive, and equitable, especially after the emergence of modern democratic societies. By the mid twentieth century, near the dawn of our current information automation revolution, libraries were the central figure in the information environment and inhabited prominent buildings in the centers of cities and college campuses. As automated information processing advanced, libraries adapted and automated many technical operations. And they have remained important places in the information environment for individual as well as collective information attention and agency. Many who wonder whether libraries have a future in an age of transformative technologies may not be aware of how library technologies and techniques have grown in sophistication over the millennia: information artifacts have expanded from cuneiform to digital tablets; information access systems have expanded from buildings to online discovery systems; information dissemination has moved from scriptoria to digital repositories; information instruction has broadened from reference assistance to digital literacies; and current automated information processing systems and human information practices are being upgraded with new AI tools and techniques. The real challenge for libraries today is to discern how best to integrate technologies that automate intelligence into structures and systems that direct these technologies to new and better ends—ends that enhance human hopes and human agency.

10 THE END OF A LIBRARY

Every library is in jeopardy of extinction within a generation. Most libraries end through neglect: an empire falls, an institution closes, heirs have other interests. Some libraries end more suddenly, when there is a natural disaster or when they become targets of war or are destroyed along with an associated group. But the death of a library is not always absolute. Libraries are regularly resurrected or re-created. Access to ancient tablets is restored in modern libraries; catalogs of older libraries are used to develop collections in new ones; texts are recovered, restored, and researched through digital libraries. This pattern of creation, destruction, and re-creation is often the historical norm. The Dead Sea Scroll Library is an example of this cycle.

In the winter of 1946/7, near a site called Khirbet Qumran along the northwest shore of the Dead Sea, Bedouin shepherds discovered a cave filled with ancient jars and scrolls. Over the next ten years, as other caves and a nearby settlement were excavated, fragments of some nine hundred manuscripts were found. In the absence of public access to these documents, which were known to be contemporaneous with Jesus of Nazareth and therefore of broad public interest, a number of fantastic theories emerged. Some conspiracy theories, claiming the suppression of scandalous scrolls, seem to have been inspired by Umberto Eco's *The Name of the Rose* (1980), in which "the monastery, and the library within it, reflect the Church's monopoly of learning." An even more fantastic claim that magical mushrooms were mentioned in the scrolls found its way into Philip K. Dick's semi-autobiographical science-fiction novel *The Transmigration of Timothy Archer* (1982). Timothy Archer, an Episcopal bishop modeled on Dick's controversial friend Bishop James Pike (1913–69), dies like Pike in the Dead Sea desert. Archer was there seeking a "mushroom [that] is Christ."

By the 1990s, careful scholarship had provided access to the texts of the scrolls. There was also a general consensus about them and the community that created and collected them, which was most likely associated with the Essene Jewish group described by Josephus as bookish, ascetic, and prophetic. At the core of this consensus is the conclusion that the Dead Sea Scrolls were from a library. Hartmut Stegemann, who describes the Qumran settlement as a "publishing house"—"to provide the numerous local Essene communities throughout the land with the manuscripts they needed for study, religious practice, and pious edification"—situates the library at the heart of the settlement. Surrounding spaces, from the adjacent reading room to the leather tannery farther out, were anchored to it. The library collection, consisting of perhaps one thousand scrolls, included books now included in Hebrew bibles, non-canonical or extra-biblical books, and books connected with the history and practices of the library's community. This last category of texts reveals details about a group called "the Yahad" or "the Community."

Around 100 BCE, the Community abandoned the Temple and its hierarchy for the wilderness, where they waited for the last days and the coming of the righteous rule of God. As members of the Community prepared for the end of history and the world, they busied themselves, "day and night," collecting, copying, studying, creating, preserving, and publishing books. The Qumran library was the physical, intellectual, and spiritual center of the Community, sustaining their collective life together. It preserved master manuscripts from which copies were made, supplied books for common and advanced study, kept archival records, and supplied writing materials. Although the concerns of the Community were universal, including the past, present, and future of the world, texts were selected and filtered through the Community's very local experiences and expectations. Their books—Hebrew leather scrolls, rather than Greek papyrus scrolls—were exclusively for their own edification. To understand these continuing sources of revelation, which to the uninitiated were "like the words of a sealed book," one needed the physical and interpretive structures that were established by the culture of the Community.

This Community was a Jewish apocalyptic sect. Between the eighth and second centuries BCE, the apocalyptic imagination emerged in Jewish prophecy as a way of exploring how rightness could be realized in and from the future when so much was wrong in the present. According to Anathea Portier-Young, the Jewish apocalyptic imagination took shape within contexts of imperialistic oppression. This apocalyptic worldview oriented "a terrorized people ... to a vision of a future ordered by divine justice." Prophetic apocalyptic visions of the past, present, and future "asserted the transience and finitude of temporal powers," "articulated a resistant counterdiscourse to the discourse of empire," and "environed, advocated, and empowered resistant action." John Collins describes the apocalyptic imagination as a particularly "scribal phenomenon," which depended on and created libraries that facilitated the uncovering of information about time.

After the Jewish-Roman wars in the first and second centuries, the Community at Qumran was gone. Before their end came, they apparently spent time working to ensure that their temporal library with its eternal knowledge would survive by hiding their collection in neighboring caves. Their final hopes for their community and library are not known. Part of their library did survive, first by being hidden for nearly two millennia. Then, after its discovery, through the careful attention of scholars it was reintroduced eventually into libraries throughout the world. Although scholarly debate continues about the scrolls and what they reveal about the world in which they were created, knowledge of this apocalyptic library and community has been restored to the historical record. This recovered library has helped religious communities that have a historical connection with the Community understand their own present hopes. AI will reveal more about the content and historical context of this library, through new forms of discovery and analysis, and people will engage with it in news ways. If surviving members of the Community did not find hope in other Jewish movements, at least their hope for the survival of their library was, in a way, realized. Libraries can become much more—and serve very different ends—than their creators initially imagine and hope.

11 THE LIBRARY AS A TRANSFORMATIVE TECHNOLOGY

In his analysis of the colonial foundations of the American university, K. Wayne Yang points out how the technologies of universities create an agency that can be turned against it, to transform the university into a decolonizing institution. Working with Donna Haraway's concept of a cyborg, which blurs the boundaries between the human body and all it encounters—including, but not limited to, technology—Yang focuses on how institutional technologies shape us and structure our agency. These systems make us structural agents or "scyborgs ... plugged in to technological grids." Although a university may begin with and exist to perpetuate "imperialist dreams of a settled world" through prescriptive curricula and policies, it cultivates forms of individual and collective agency in learners that can be used to disassemble imperial technologies and reassemble them for alternative futures.

Focusing on Indigenous and Black histories, Yang describes a movement within universities that is both a rejection of present powers and an affirmation of deeper sources of wisdom. The university is a set of technologies, each designed for a particular end. Understood this way, it is possible to figure out and forecast how these technologies will operate—and then develop subversive strategies to redirect them. Against the force of "settler futurity, which is always nostalgic for its current power," technologies can be appropriated for radical transformative projects. These projects are neither dystopian nor utopian. They turn away from imperial fears and false hopes, recognizing that the technologies integrated into our lives can be used for the realizations of a better world.

The libraries of the serial empires of the ancient world created limited forms of structural agency, but their necessary openness to the future meant they were never as constrained as their communities. The futures they anticipated were never fully realized, but there was a future and they participated in it in surprising ways. Their records were preserved, their books were copied, and their ideas were kept alive. Although early Christian libraries were targeted frequently during Roman persecutions, in the end Christian libraries saved the textual culture of Roman civilization. The works of Cicero, Seneca, and others were kept peacefully in monastery libraries, which were the central sites for book production, collection, and circulation in Europe for centuries following the collapse of the Roman Empire. Later, after their so-called rediscovery during the Renaissance, such texts became cornerstones of libraries and literary cultures.

Within the last few hundred years, as literacy, literary materials, and libraries increased significantly, modern libraries have created more extensive forms of structural agency, which have transformed the users of libraries as well as libraries themselves. Libraries are a type of transformative technology for individuals and societies. For academic libraries, an important turning point arrived with the development of libraries to support the research university model. Reacting to a loss of authority and agency in the overloaded information environment of the Enlightenment, German reformers organized the pedagogical and scholarly technologies of the university to form people who would engage with knowledge in disciplined ways. University libraries moved intellectually—and often physically—to the center of campuses, providing resources, services, and spaces necessary for the formation of scholarly agency. These libraries made possible other forms of agency as well, which is why Yang says his scyborg "can often be caught in the basement library" of the university. Ta-Nehisi Coates, who says he was enrolled at Howard University but formed by the related institution "The Mecca," found the university library—instead of the classroom—"open, unending, free."

The significant turning point in library history for those outside of academic institutions came with the public library movement in the mid nineteenth century. In the United States, generations since then have valued their public libraries for providing useful information, public spaces, and transformative reading experiences. Modeled on the social libraries of the late eighteenth and early nineteenth centuries, which emphasized "useful knowledge," leaders of the public library movement saw themselves as cultural caretakers and sought to perpetuate dominant social values. While this was somewhat effective, Wayne Wiegand points to the more interesting history of how the diverse cultures public libraries served ended up shaping American public libraries. Public libraries initially focused on providing resources, services, and spaces for "self-education agency," but what the vast majority of readers wanted from their libraries was access to popular fiction—not only for entertainment, but also because it empowered "white women, people of color, and the lower classes to rethink societal roles others assigned to them" and to "imagine different social environments and situations." The public got what it wanted from their libraries, librarianship diversified, and public libraries now have an established reputation of being able "to satisfy self-designed needs of multiple groups and at the same time help individuals make sense of their worlds in myriad ways."

The intentions with which a library begins, which influence the subsequent work of selection and mediation, can be changed, broadened, and subverted. Sometimes books and libraries are targeted for destruction to demoralize a society and demolish its culture. Thus the great city of Tenochtitlan, the capital of the Aztec Empire, was conquered by the Spanish and its books and libraries were systematically destroyed. Colonists and missionaries often brought chests of books with them, and libraries were among the first institutions established in their settlements. Once libraries are established, though, they often fail to function as oppressive institutions only—there is too much human agency released through reading, reflection, writing, and the discovery of greater hopes in and through libraries. In the United States, librarianship began as a conservative profession: library leader Melvil Dewey, philanthropist Andrew Carnegie, and others believed the public library was an agent of social reform conforming to their cultural expectations. Today, the reformative role of libraries takes a much more inclusive approach toward personal and social transformation. We may disagree about what should be included in libraries, but we should be able to agree on the importance of institutions that enable the flourishing of the human imagination and hope—including from unanticipated sources. With AI, we face an information overload challenge exponentially greater than the conditions created by the printing press. We need libraries and librarians to leverage AI to manage information—including information generated by AI—that truly augments human attention and agency. We also need people, within and outside of libraries, critiquing how we integrate AI into our systems and services for a better future. Shannon Vallor says that the "true soul of technology is not efficiency but generosity; it is the gift of a future." Throughout history, the library—often in spite of its leaders, supporters, and detractors—has been a transformative technology, enabling all of us to imagine and create with generosity a better world through the new forms of structural agency it creates for us.

12 THE INDUSTRIAL IMAGINATION

Marshall McLuhan said the printing press was "the blueprint of all mechanization to follow." Standardizing text through set type, and the production of multiple copies of that text through repeated impressions of type onto sheets of paper by hand—about two hundred per hour—prefigured what would be possible when mechanisms designed for uniform and multiple outputs could be powered by energy sources not directly dependent on human-generated power. During the nineteenth century, the blueprint became a reality—not only for printing presses, but for many other means of production. The steam-powered press, capable of more than two thousand automated impressions per hour, was trialed in 1812. The nineteenth century quickly became "a vast matrix" of new technologies and related techniques. This matrix included machines such as telegraphs and trains; skills such as coding and engineering; raw materials and manufactured infrastructures, such as telegraph cables and railroad tracks; social conventions represented by standardized forms and schedules; cultures associated with communication and travel; and political systems enabling nationalism and colonialism.

Some wondered about the value and values of humans in increasingly complex industrial societies. Fyodor Dostoevsky, through the unnamed anti-hero in *Notes from Underground*, offered one critique in the 1860s. Underground man—a former bureaucrat at a civil information agency, in the "abstract and intentional city" of Saint Petersburg—questions the methodology and metrics of his aspiring industrial society. Can human potential be realized fully through science and technology? If so, he reasons, "all that is needed is to discover the laws of nature," classify and calculate all human actions, "and all possible questions will disappear." "And then the Crystal Palace will arise," underground man continues, "halcyon days will arrive." Life may become "dreadfully boring (for what's the point of doing anything if all is set and classified according to graphs and tables?). On the other hand, though, everything will be extremely reasonable." For underground man, something is left out of this cold calculus—an irreducible and insatiable desire. This desire, for a love that leads to a new and fuller life, "is constantly knocking all systems and theories to hell."

The Crystal Palace to which Dostoevsky referred housed the first world exhibition in 1851. This "Great Exhibition of the Industry of All Nations" in London showcased the technological accomplishments of the industrial revolution. The Crystal Palace did not merely exhibit the ability of new technologies to create a better world; it demonstrated—through displays of raw materials, machinery, and manufacturing—new divisions of labor and mechanisms for generating new sources of wealth. Jonathon Shears describes the Great Exhibition as "a watershed moment in the development of modern-day consumer habits ... the first outburst of the phantasmagoria of commodity culture." The automation of agency presented was not concerned ultimately with human industry or potential, but rather commercial industry and profitability. This was a vision of the world in which everything is predictable to be purchasable. Dostoevsky called the Crystal Palace "an apocalyptic nightmare of a sort of the Tower of Babel." At the exhibition, he wrote, masses saw a potential escape from the rigid oppression of the present "in the name of utopia on earth, by a mechanical, all-pervasive system." Dostoevsky, however, saw in these new systems new forms of oppression.

The industrial revolution remade the United States into a new political and economic empire. After destroying and displacing numerous and diverse Indigenous settlements, by 1900 an agrarian nation of east coast villages had become a nation of states and territories connecting the western and eastern coasts of North America and reaching beyond them. Describing the industrial origins of higher education in the United States, Arthur Levine and Scott Van Pelt describe a nation that was "built of steel, powered by petroleum and electricity, illuminated by gas and electric lights, and crisscrossed by railroad, telegraph, and telephone lines." During this industrial transformation, a few "industrial natives"—"born after the advent of canals, steamboats, factories, railroads, and farm technologies"—consolidated technological innovations and wealth by creating financial empires: "Andrew Carnegie in steel, John D. Rockefeller in oil, Jay Gould in railroads, and J. P. Morgan in banking." The power these men had over the country was significant and led to price-fixing, deplorable conditions for workers, and other unjust practices. It also shaped the nation's institutions through industrial wealth, goals, and methods.

Various types of libraries—private subscription and circulating libraries as well as public and national libraries—proliferated during the nineteenth century to support a growing reading public's desire for "recreation, information, and social advancement." Academic libraries grew, too, in both size and complexity to keep up with new discoveries and advances in knowledge. The public library movement in the United States was advanced significantly in the late nineteenth century by the philanthropy of Carnegie, who provided grants to communities to build over fifteen hundred public library buildings across the country. As inspiring as these buildings were meant to be, they were designed for efficiency of access and service. They also primarily existed to support participation in the industrial system. Still, they provided intellectual resources and physical spaces for critiquing the status quo and creating alternative worlds. In an 1848 plea for more American libraries, to fight "infidelity and Romanism" in the West, Noah Porter, professor and later president at Yale, wrote about hopes—greater than he could imagine—which might be realized through a library: "Not a day passes in which [a library] may not give a stimulus to some noble spirit, and wake his intellect and his heart to a new and glorious life."

The innovations of the nineteenth century secured the dominance of print. Steam-powered presses produced mass quantities of books and other printed materials, and railways formed efficient distribution networks. Technologies such as the telegraph and the telephone provided new and more immediate means of communication, but they did not provide substantial alternatives to the imaginative world of books or libraries. The industrial imagination and the dominance of print had a long legacy, even as new information and communication technologies proliferated throughout the twentieth century and created new information resources and communication methods. Some of these newer information technologies enabled new forms of efficiency, such as the automation of many technical library operations, and new AI technologies promise even more. But the more interesting work of libraries and librarians in our late industrial age, including with AI, continues to be in supporting and enabling the less efficient but more essential qualities of human intelligence—those capabilities that enable us to reflect on our reality, imagine new possibilities, and create something new.

13 ARCHIVAL FEVERS

At the opening of the Freud Museum in 1994, Jacques Derrida delivered a long lecture titled "The Concept of the Archive: A Freudian Impression." The talk was later published as a short book, *Archive Fever: A Freudian Impression*. In his lecture and book, Derrida attempts to deconstruct the concept of the archive by exploring the interrelated dynamics of the natural, psychological archive (the "memorial archive") and the artificial, technological archive (the "scriptural archive"). For Derrida, the archive includes a physical place, such as the Freud Museum, but he was more interested in the *process* of archiving that creates such sites—the process of documentation—and in what archived traces forget, remember, and defer.

Derrida says, "We are in need of archives" because we are "burning with a [fever]." This is a very Freudian fever for Derrida, involving the precarious balancing of drives for both life and death—competing compulsions to save as well as destroy. Driven by a sense of finitude and the possibility of forgetfulness, we inscribe and then consign a trace to an external location, an archive. But once the trace is externalized, it is at risk of being destroyed. Derrida claims that institutional archives inherit our psychological desires for both transcendence and annihilation, and therefore are intrinsically unstable.

Another Freudian concept Derrida brings to the concept of the archive is "retrospective causality." Derrida says that "the archive doesn't simply record the past." He says the question of what an archive is, is not exclusively a question of the past: "It is a question of the future, the question of the future itself, the question of a response, of a promise and of a responsibility for tomorrow … if we want to know what [the archive] will have meant, we will only know in times to come. Perhaps." Derrida describes how the archive grows by incorporating new knowledge into it: "the archive augments itself, engrosses itself, it gains in *auctoritas*."

Yet the ongoing accumulation of knowledge, contributed by those who use the archive, means that the archive's *auctoritas* or authority is not absolute. The archive defers meaning and is never closed: "It opens out of the future." Derrida emphasizes the "potentially transformative capacity" for new interpretations. The archive—all that is gathered and guarded, however imperfectly—is, as Francis Blouin and William Rosenberg say, a "place of uncovering" that opens up the past, present, and future.

In a digression, Derrida refers to an "archival earthquake" caused by electronic media, but he defers this discussion for the most part. Some years after the publication of *Archive Fever*, Derrida was wondering if all our new machines were creating a different type of archive fever. He saw that the process of archivization—the "institutional passage from the private to the public"—was breaking down. "What circulates on the internet," he said, "belongs to an automatic space of publication: the public/private distinction is increasingly being wiped out." The archive becomes everything, and a new unnamed fever reigns over it. Here we see the place and need for institutional interventions, for concrete archives that join automation with selection. As the end of Derrida's life approached, he was anxious for his own personal archive to end up in "a safe, institutional place." He worried that, outside of an institutional archives, "everything he wrote would simply disappear after he was gone."

Derrida's musings on the archive—as something unstable, incomplete, open, and changing with digital technologies—surface three major characteristics of institutional archives. First, archives represent an attempt to negate time. Time, which Marc Bloch described as "an irreversible onward rush," is an annihilating force and a dimension of our "fever" to communicate "across the barriers of time, distance, and experience." Second, linking and mediating between the past, present, and future, the archive is a repository of human temporality—of time "lived or to be lived," in the words of Manuel Castells—which can enrich our understanding and experience of time. As Blouin and Rosenberg point out, archives are sites of ongoing temporal revelation—of "imagination, creativity, production, as well as of documentary preservation." Third, if they are to endure and be accessible—especially over the long term—archives must be curated through intentional design, proactive selection, and managed access over time. The archive depends on institutions that possess what W. Boyd Rayward describes as a "commitment to time," particularly to the future. Future researchers will have to answer the question that Bloch challenges historians to answer in every historical book "worthy of the name": "How can I know what I am about to say?"

A theoretical concern about transcending time, to understand it better, leads to a technical need for managing the archive in and through time. These are ancient insights concerning ancient impulses, but now, with increasingly sophisticated digital technologies, we are confronted with a new and challenging archive that is prolific, dispersed, and fragile. With the advent of generative AI, which can facilitate conversations with our archives through prompts, we also can speak of a new type of archival fever that is adding to our scriptural archive but is less directly linked with our memorial archive. In addition to content automatically captured for the archive and potentially for institutional archives, the archive is now burgeoning with automatically created content. For the technical scriptural archive to remain relevant to and for humans, humans will have to design archives with AI that can continue to check, capture, and change time—and keep archives and libraries open to new human futures.

14 ON INEXACTITUDE IN LIBRARIES

"On Exactitude in Science" is a one-paragraph story published by Jorge Luis Borges in 1946. It begins with an ellipsis: " ... In that Empire, the Art of Cartography attained such Perfection that the map of a single Province occupied the entirety of the City." The ambitious imperial cartographers eventually designed a complete map of the empire that was equal in size to it, coinciding with it at every point. Subsequent generations, "not so fond of the Study of Cartography ... saw that that vast map was Useless." Left unattended, only tattered ruins survived "inhabited by Animals and Beggars." Elsewhere, "in all the Land there is no other Relic of the Disciplines of Geography." The attempt to create a complete representative map of the empire was not only futile but "unconscionable," asserts the story's narrator. The accomplishments of the empire, gone by the end of the paragraph, become useless and forgotten.

In an earlier short story, "Tlön, Uqbar, Orbis Tertius" (1940), Borges narrates the discovery of a world that initially exists in an encyclopedia fabricated by a secret society. Over time, through books and artifacts, the imaginary Tlön begins to break into the material world of the story. For Borges, who both labored and luxuriated in libraries, the archive was a foundational metaphor. Through his creative explorations of the relationship between representation and reality, Borges reminds us that the library as an archive, conceptually and concretely, is neither complete nor inviolable. Neither is it absolutely determinative. Ursula K. Le Guin's postapocalyptic novel *Always Coming Home* is structured as an archive of the future—or, more precisely, a future. But it is an incomplete archive; no source documents the apocalypse. An opening note acknowledges the challenge of translating texts that do not yet exist, but also notes, "The past, after all, can be quite as obscure as the future."

Le Guin says, "we make the world we inhabit." This includes the archive—the material traces of the past, from rocks to records—for "we must have a past to make a future with." But the archive, incomplete and independently insufficient, must be created, cultivated, and interpreted with care. If we ignore or approach it with violence, we "run the risk of losing or destroying what in fact is." Those who think they have discovered or created a new world often find themselves living in a lost world—ceded or unceded, by treaty or violence. The alternative is to participate in what is. In the "Carrier Bag Theory of Fiction," Le Guin describes two ancient artifacts and narratives. One artifact is the arrow, which produces the "killer story"—the "Techno-Heroic" undertaking, "Herculean, Promethean, conceived as triumph, hence ultimately as tragedy." It is the story of Cain, empire, conquest, the nuclear bomb, and killer machines.

The other artifact, perhaps the more ancient cultural device, is the container—the tool made to bring things home. The sack or bag is the natural figure and shape of "the life story ... Myths of creation and transformation, trickster stories, folktales, jokes, novels." "A book holds words," Le Guin says, and words "bear meanings." Stories discovered in or added to the archive will include conflict. But, Le Guin warns, "the reduction of narrative to conflict is absurd":

> Conflict, competition, stress, struggle, etc., within the narrative conceived as carrier bag / belly / box / house / medicine bundle, may be seen as necessary elements of a whole which itself cannot be characterized either as conflict or harmony, since its purpose is neither resolution nor stasis but continuing process.

A library is a carrier bag of culture, containing books that individually and collectively provide us with sources about how we understand and misunderstand continuity and change—and how we participate in these processes. Like one of Le Guin's books, a library is a resource that functions as "a way of trying to describe what is in fact going on, what people actually do and feel, how people relate to everything else in this vast sack, the belly of the universe, this womb of things to be and tomb of things that were, this unending story."

In an earlier work, I proposed a sources continuum that assesses the primacy of sources through dimensions of time and transformation. After years of trying to teach undergraduate students to work with contradictory historical sources, I gave up on the false dichotomy of primary versus secondary sources—a frail construct that required too many qualifications. So, I would select a controversial event (e.g., the

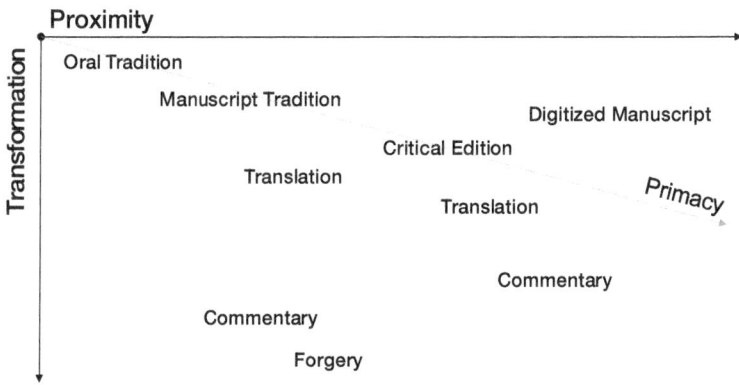

FIGURE 14.1 Sources Continuum. Diagram by the author

killing of a group of missionaries in the early nineteenth century) or a complex life (e.g., the life of Jesus in the first century) and literally spread out sources (or surrogates) on a table. I asked students to arrange these along two axes: one related to proximity to the event; the other related to the extent to which the text may have been modified through biases, editors, errors, and manipulators. Full knowledge of the event or a life was impossible. We only had witnesses, with varying degrees of accuracy and credibility, pointing toward the inaccessible point of origin of those two lines.

To understand the usefulness and limits of the library as an archive requires nuanced understandings of what we know (evidence) as well as how we know what we know (epistemology). It also requires humility about what we can know and do. Our sources for understanding reality, created in specific times and places with imperfect information, require contextualization, interpretation, and care. Libraries do not simply preserve the raw materials of history. Through their interpretive works—of classification, description, transcription, translation, instruction, presentation, et cetera—they aim to mediate possibilities of meaning. These creative attempts may, at times, seem to add up to a coherent, complete, and durable map of the world. But Le Guin reminds us that any creative work is only a sketch-map or a "chart of shorelines on a foggy coast." Yet incomplete sources, mediated through libraries, are necessary for understanding our world and imagining more complete and better ones. Libraries provide world-modeling and world-making sources for hope—and, as Le Guin says, "one does not get on without hope."

PART THREE

THE LIBRARY AS A SITE OF ANTICIPATION: HOW LIBRARIES ARE SIGNS OF HOPE

N   Fine Arts

P   Language and Literature

15 THE ANTILIBRARY

The Argentine writer (and librarian) Jorge Luis Borges regularly returned to two images from antiquity: the Tower of Babel, signifying chaos and fragmentation, and the Library of Alexandria, signifying order and unity. Many discussions of his short story "The Library of Babel" miss the interplay between these two images in the text, focusing on the concept of the library while missing the more powerful dynamic of the specter of Babel. "The Library of Babel" is not a proposal for a total library, a concept Borges described in a 1939 essay as "a subaltern horror." "The fancy or the imagination or the utopia of the Total Library has certain characteristics that are easily confused with virtues," Borges begins this essay. He explains that if everything that could possibly be written were, the resulting library would be of "astronomical size." Its inhuman scale, which only chance could organize, would be useless. Everything would be there, "but for every sensible line or accurate fact there would be millions of meaningless cacophonies, verbal farragoes, and babblings." All the generations of humankind "could pass before the dizzying shelves [could] ever reward them with a tolerable page."

In "The Library of Babel," published two years later in 1941, Borges created a world called "the Library" that amplifies the horrific idea of a total library. This universe consists of interconnected galleries and shelves, which are uniform in appearance and seem infinite in number. There is no center or periphery. The books on the shelves reveal nothing meaningful, and the Library is an object of endless and fruitless speculation. When the denizens of the Library, the "librarians," realize that it contains all books—including those with meaning, purpose, and justification—their "first reaction was unbounded joy." But "unbridled hopefulness" was eventually followed "by similarly disproportionate depression." For the Library contained *everything*: "the faithful catalog of the Library, thousands and thousands of false catalogs, the proof of the falsity of those false catalogs, a proof of the falsity of the true catalog." Most books are meaningless, filled with letters that very rarely form words. Among the sparse books that might contain coherent text, most of it would be false. This is not a library but an antilibrary—the antithesis of a library—void of intention, selection, and mediation. The image of Babel negates the image of Alexandria, a vision of access to good, true, and valuable information.

In "The Memory Librarian" by Janelle Monáe and Alaya Dawn Johnson, a character named Seshet with the title "Director Librarian" manages the memories of her city to maintain a kind of peace. This peace has nothing to do with reconciliation and wholeness; it involves erasure and suppression. The ruling order, New Dawn, promises—"to the right kind of citizens"—"beauty in order, peace in rigidity, and tranquility in a constant, sun-dappled present." Seshet, named for the Egyptian goddess of the written word, is a "Memory Librarian" who unwrites personal histories and divergent thoughts. As curator of "the proper flow of pure, fresh memory," she is in actuality an anti-librarian—attempting to inhibit attention and agency. While the old totalitarian trick of changing the meaning of a word to control thought is obvious, in the story—as in reality—the truth within the society's Memory Repository cannot be controlled by an anti-librarian, even if it exists within what can be called an antilibrary. Monáe says, "Beyond time and memory—where the computer cannot reach—is dreaming." Greater and more powerful truths and hopes transcend our fear-management systems.

The inherent flaw in creating an antilibrary and practicing anti-librarianship is explored in Karl Schroeder's short story "Noon in the Antilibrary." Set in a world of fake news and deepfakes, in which language is used to gain power rather than communicate meaning—a world, alas, too similar to ours—the US military builds an antilibrary to fight false information with false information. The antilibrary consists of a digital collection of source materials that can be used to re-create any possible text or event. It was "a tool that could produce a literal library's worth of entirely bogus material: videos, articles, subtly nonsensical books cross-referenced and supported by other nonsensical books—a true antilibrary—and do it faster than the news cycle, or even social media, could keep up." But a functioning world, and the complex systems that support it, depends on "accurate data at all scales for it to run." You can lie about the cargo on trains and where they are going, but deliveries have to be scheduled, actual destinations have to be communicated, and engines need to receive clear directions and interact with other devices. Truth is inescapable. Even in a convincing alternative reality generated by an antilibrary, facts and accurate testaments run through its content and systems. These fundamental truths provide a way out of—and lead to the end of—the antilibrary in the story, but also in reality.

A helpful lesson from "The Library of Babel" is a prophetic warning about an internet augmented with apparent information generated by large language models that lack understanding or restraint. Like the Total Library, the internet—the global network facilitating the transmission of digital information between connected devices—is an artificial entity, increasingly interacting with artificial agents, which seems infinite in content and form. Like Borges's antilibrary, an AI-augmented internet *might* provide access to "all that is able to be expressed, in every language." But Borges's narrator could have written about such a version of the internet what he wrote about the Library of Babel, which ends with the bleak hope of finding order in disorder:

> Like all the people of the Library [internet], in my younger days I traveled [surfed]; I have journeyed [surfed] in quest of a book [information], perhaps the catalog of catalogs [the automated summary of all automatically summarized search results]. Now that my eyes can hardly make out what I myself have written [typed], I am preparing to die. ... My solitude is cheered by the elegant hope that if an eternal traveler [surfer] should journey in any direction [click on any link], the traveler [surfer] would find after untold centuries that the same volumes [data] are repeated in the same disorder—which, repeated, become order: the Order.

The intentional antilibrary is self-contradictory. Because its sole method and strategy—falsehood—depends on truth, such diabolical distortions are doomed. More perplexing are unintentional or self-forming antilibraries, aided by a more autonomous internet, which can endure for a time without intention. But they are doomed as well, especially as their limited models of the world become more ungrounded from and less representative of the real world. To create a library is to attempt to impose a provisional and correctable order on the world—or, better, to provide refined means for interpreting the world—so that we may understand it, engage with it, and change it. A library can transcend human limits, augmenting what we can know, hope for, and do. But it remains a human creation that, like us, is imperfect, corruptible, finite, and ever in need of improvement. At the end of *The Divine Comedy*, in the light of eternity, Dante sees not a total library but a total book:

> In its depth I saw contained,
> by love into a single volume bound,
> the leaves scattered through the universe.

That unity exists only in *Paradiso*, glimpsed at the end of long labyrinthine journey that began outside of *The Inferno* with the poet Virgil. The library helped form that labyrinth, filled with the books of Virgil and others, to which Dante added his own to help others find meaning in their journeys through the world.

16 THE APOCALYPTIC IMAGINATION

Imagining the end of the world is an ancient human practice—perhaps one of the most ancient. Often caught up with our origin stories, we create narratives to understand why the world exists as is does, or at all, and what might become of it and us. The archive of our anticipations runs deep in time and grows daily, often—and especially now—accelerated by significant technological changes. In 1516, as new lands and people were being encountered by European explorers, Thomas More created the term "utopia." Utopia can mean a good (*eu-*) and/or no (*ou-*) place (*-topos*), and the term is used regularly to describe visions for different places and futures. To the linguistic ambiguity of the word is added ambivalence about specific examples of utopias, including More's *Utopia*. "Every utopia since Utopia," Ursula K. Le Guin observes, "has also been, clearly or obscurely, actually or possibly, in the author's or in the readers' judgment, both a good place and a bad one [*dustopos*]. Every eutopia contains a dystopia, every dystopia contains a eutopia." There is another and more ancient term that in concerned with imagining alternative and more hope-filled places and times: "apocalyptic."

When Jewish prophets began declaring "the end" some three millennia ago, they were concerned with local, near, and this-worldly ends. As their concerns broadened to include greater political powers such as the Babylonian Empire, which displaced many peoples from their lands, their expectations of "the end" became more cosmic, distant, and otherworldly. The apocalyptic imagination—a confluence of Jewish as well as Babylonian, Persian, and Hellenistic influences—emerged as a way of exploring how rightness could be realized when so much was wrong in the present. While the term apocalyptic is often reduced to something akin to dystopic, focusing on visions of cataclysmic chaos, the ancient apocalyptic imagination sought to uncover hidden or deeper dimensions of knowledge, space, time, and agency to discover a narrative about a new and better world.

The most famous or infamous apocalyptic text, considered to be an exemplar of this ancient genre, is the Book of Revelation or the Apocalypse of John. The Apocalypse of John is a circular letter to seven first-century churches, revealing through dramatic images that two spiritual cities are present in every city. One of these cities, called Babylon, is manifested in the imperial city of Rome. John announces that this evil city is doomed and falling, and that the good city of God—New Jerusalem—is arriving and will be established permanently. The good end that John announces is meant to inspire both hope and action in his readers and hearers, but the necessary and enigmatic images associated with the annihilation of evil leave many modern readers confused and fearful. The wild writer Hunter S. Thompson said the Apocalypse was one of his "favorite pieces of writing": he loved "the wild power of the language and the purity of the madness that governs it and makes it music."

In ancient apocalyptic literature, written to reveal what was hidden, books are both means of and metaphors for apocalypse. In John's Apocalypse, John says he was directed to write a book about what was revealed to him and to send it to the churches in Asia Minor. After writing seven epistles to seven churches, John writes about a vision of a sealed book in the form of a scroll, and his narrative advances as its seals are broken. Before the visions associated with the seals end, John is told to stop writing and he sees another scroll. He is told to eat it; not everything is revealed. The visions continue, and at a final judgment scene more books are opened, and people are judged according to what is recorded in them. There is also the "book of life," in which names of the saved were written before the creation of the world. John's book of books depended on actual libraries, especially the books included in the Hebrew Bible, and his imagery becomes more coherent when these antecedent texts are known.

The apocalyptic imagination, whether focusing on the absolute end of the world or the end of the world as we know it, experienced a modern resurgence following the industrial revolutions. Since Mary Shelley's *Frankenstein* (1818) and *The Last Man* (1826), technological progress has fueled a range of fears about civilizational decline or collapse. After the advent of nuclear and AI technologies in the mid twentieth century, apocalyptic books, films, and thinking proliferated and are now commonplace and fill our libraries. These fictional works and worlds have profoundly shaped our hopes and fears about AI. Indeed, much of our public discourse about AI has more to do with science fiction than computer science. Prominent among apocalyptic fears is the loss of accumulated knowledge. Libraries, as institutions responsible for preserving sources of and structures for knowledge, often figure prominently in apocalyptic literature signifying the loss of knowledge—or, in more hopeful scenarios, its recovery, re-creation, or creation.

In the original Apocalypse, we can imagine Roman and other libraries functioning in first-century cities as servile and deformative agents of imperial oppression or—alternatively—as subversive and transformative agents of liberation. In the Apocalypse, when the imperial city Babylon falls—"the great city that rules over the rulers of the earth"—we see the rulers of the earth fleeing the condemned city with whatever is good, and bringing these goods into New Jerusalem. Good work and works, including technical skills and technologies, survive the fall. When Rome fell a few centuries later, the Roman senator Cassiodorus saved books from sacked libraries to be added to a new library for a new community. Beyond the end of the world as we know it, as we seek renewed and new cities, libraries can be a point of continuity and change, providing sources, signs, and structures for both. We cannot build New Jerusalem on our own, the Apocalypse reveals, but we are capable of doing and building good things that will survive the fall of all our Babylons. Libraries and librarians are indispensable agents of transformation in this great work of hope.

17 LIBRARIES OF BABYLON

Libraries can be instruments of empire, but many dystopian visions recognize their inherent anti-imperialistic potential and destabilizing power. When Aldous Huxley visited the United States in the 1920s, he thought he had glimpsed the future—and he hated it. The future he imagined in connection with his visit was, in many ways, prophetic: Huxley saw clearly how the logic of the industrial imagination would create and deploy advanced technologies to eliminate inefficiency, "the [unforgivable] sin against the Holy Ghost." His novel *Brave New World* (1932) presents a dystopia based on Huxley's assessment of American progress and its trajectory. In this new industrial world, through technological engineering, "human invention" has triumphed over wild nature: life is genetically predetermined, educationally conditioned, and materially comfortable. History and literature, full of "so many unpleasant things," are suppressed. Science is reduced to focusing on "the most immediate problems of the moment." But some desire a braver, older world. One, awakened in part by a forbidden library, demands: "I don't want comfort. I want God, I want poetry, I want real danger, I want freedom, I want goodness. I want sin. ... I'm claiming the right to be unhappy." Books are chief among his consolations.

A controlled and closed archive may be safer than an open library, but the unarchived can be heard in silent voids and noisy lies. The amount of work to manage the archive in George Orwell's *Nineteen Eighty-Four* (1949), for example, is substantial. Indeed, technological progress must be arrested and mostly used to control life through pseudo information and thought control, constant video surveillance, and perpetual war. As the Ministry of Peace maintains constant war conditions, resulting in poverty over plentitude and ignorance over intelligence, the Ministry of Truth wages a war against words. In addition to organizing lies, this ministry destroys words to destroy thought, making it hard to articulate and imagine dissent. It hunts down, destroys, and continuously rewrites old books. Thus, the books that do exist are completely untrustworthy. The past is regularly erased and the future circumscribed: history becomes a palimpsest, continuously "scraped clean and reinscribed" for a futurity that perpetuates current power. It is a momentous and monstrous effort. But "reality control" constantly meets resistance, with which the Ministry of Love must contend brutally. An inordinate amount of attention and time must be given to frustrate the hopes of one man who begins a personal journal for an "imagined future" and a different world.

In Ray Bradbury's *Fahrenheit 451*, written in the UCLA library in the 1940s and published in 1953, most people have been convinced to live without books and libraries. Instead, they settle for simpler visual communications delivered through new technologies. Choosing to live in a world without memory or meaningful words, the public stop reading books and books become a threat to what a majority in society accept as peace. Books do not agree with each other, one antagonist points out: a library is a Tower of Babel. The protagonist Montag is not at all happy in this world. He begins to wonder what is in books, why people would live and die for them, and he seeks to learn what they are for. One character informs him: "Books were only one type of receptacle where we stored a lot of things we were afraid we might forget ... they stitched patches of the universe together into one garment for us." As the world without books nears its end, Montag finds his way into a community of "book people" who form a living library. Reversing the shift from oral to written literacy, people memorize and become books—keeping the knowledge the community thinks it "will need intact and safe" for and in a better world. Montag himself becomes the books of Ecclesiasticus and the Apocalypse.

We often learn the value of the library through its negation; only in its absence do we recognize it as an indispensable resource for hope. When the Time Traveler in H. G. Wells's *The Time Machine* (1895) arrives in the distant future, he finds our world in "ruinous splendor"—not the advanced civilization other futuristic utopian books had led him to expect. In an abandoned palace of green porcelain, he finds galleries of history, science, and technology. One gallery reminds him of "a military chapel hung with tattered flags," but he soon realizes that these are the "decaying vestiges" of a library. In a world in which all complex institutions and aspirations "have been swept out of existence," this "sombre wilderness of rotting paper" seems a testament to an "enormous waste of labour." The technologies that remain, in the mechanical Underworld, represent a dark "triumph over Nature"—including humanity. In the underground machine world, there is little thought outside of habit. Wells, who wrote additional utopias (and dystopias) with the hope of reforming his present world, has his narrator suggest that the Time Traveler's story is cautionary.

In P. D. James's novel *The Children of Men* (1992), the end of human history advances in a world without children. Yet nations continue to develop their libraries and archives for readers they can only imagine. As much as the people in this aging world try to live in the present, this is insufficient. Finding some reassurance in the centuries-long cultural record of their past, they transfer their hope in the future to a record that will survive them. But this escape from their constricted temporality is pursued with the awareness that their books and manuscripts likely will not be read but return to dust—like them, but later. The narrator, skeptical of the effort, acknowledges the human need for hope. "Man is diminished if he lives without knowledge of his past," he says, but "without hope of a future he becomes a beast ... the loss of that hope, [is] the end of science and invention." He, too, keeps a diary, even if neither he nor the words will survive. But the need to capture, understand, and project his experiences into the future—even if it is uninhabited—is irrepressible.

John Milton claimed books "have a potency of life in them": "Books are not absolutely dead things, but do contain a potency of life in them to be as active as that soul was whose progeny they are ... they do preserve as in a vial the purest efficacy and extraction of that living intellect that bred them." Books inherit human agency, but they also have an artificial agency of their own. The same is true of libraries, which blend human and artificial agency in ways that are instructive for how best to integrate new types of artificial agency into our lives and world. Libraries are far from absolutely dead entities. As both an idea and a material reality, library agency consistently survives inattention, suppression, and destruction. Kate Crawford, Rachel Adams, Karen Hao, and others describe structural threats of new empires of AI—new modalities of power, extraordinary concentrations of resources across space and time, and inequitable benefits and impacts—which libraries can help us understand, resist, reform, and replace. Our commitment to libraries can be described as an absurd act of faith. The writer Alberto Manguel, who like Jorge Louis Borges served for a time as the Director of the National Library of

Argentina, opens his book *The Library at Night* with a reflection on the futility of our commitment to the library:

> with bewildering optimism, we continue to assemble whatever scraps of information we can gather in scrolls and books and computer chips, on shelf after library shelf, whether material, virtual or otherwise, pathetically intent on lending the world a semblance of sense and order, while knowing perfectly well that, however much we'd like to believe the contrary, our pursuits are doomed to failure.

For Manguel, the Library of Alexandria is as futile, ultimately, as the misdirected ambitions behind the Tower of Babel. And yet he believes libraries are important places "for future readers to find clues in order to imagine better worlds." It is not optimism that Manguel observes but hope—reasonable hope, rather than temperamental optimism—which is practiced and cultivated as a virtue. As a virtue, hope is not merely a feeling about or an assertion of a preferred future: the practice and discipline of hope explores and orients us toward desirable futures informed by what is good, true, and beautiful. Hope energizes us to work for better futures. The ruins of Babel and Babylon, real and imagined, provide negative clues for better futures. But the idea of the Library of Alexandria, rather than its lost ruins or ruinous past, provides more positive clues about why we may be convinced of the transformative potential and power of libraries.

FIGURE 17.1 Vancouver (BC) Public Library's Central Branch, 2023, which regularly appears in sci-fi shows (photographed by the author)

18 LIBRARIES OF NEW ATLANTIS

Libraries function as signs of hope in utopian as well as dystopian visions of the future. In his seventeenth-century "fable" *New Atlantis*, Francis Bacon imagined a utopian society dedicated to scientific discovery, technological innovation, and the liberating power of knowledge. The discovery of this good place on the island of Bensalem, which could be translated as "son of (Jeru)salem or peace," is introduced allusively as a realization of divine new creation: "as in the beginning ... [God] would now discover land to us, that we might not perish." At the center of Bacon's ideal society is Salomon's House. This research center, with massive and diverse facilities for studying natural phenomena and creating artificial works, functions to understand the world, to enlarge "the bounds of Human Empire," and to effect "all things possible." New Atlantis is not the New Jerusalem of the Apocalypse. It is, however, a significant realization of it, showing how humans may participate in the transformation of the world through their work and works.

Bacon was among the first modern thinkers to bring scientific discovery and technological work together, making the latter a valued application of the former. Both, Bacon argued, had critical roles in restoring what had been lost in humanity's primordial fall from initial creation or its loss of paradise. Technological advances such as the printing press, gunpowder, and the compass, Bacon argued, had made possible a new age of learning, peace, and exploration in Europe. This new age required more rigorous methods for advancing knowledge that overcame flawed faculties, limited perspectives and experiences, and received dogmas and superstitions. The resources necessary for the advancement of learning and society—rooted in hopes for creating a better world—included people such as teachers and researchers, places such as libraries and laboratories, and resources such as books and scientific equipment.

While Bacon was right that humans are capable of growing in knowledge, he was too optimistic about a peace that could be realized through modern publications, weaponry, and exploration. Indeed, all these innovations are implicated in enhancing the scale of religious and political violence in the centuries that followed their introduction into the West. Michel Foucault warned that utopian visions can close in on themselves; the technologically enhanced house of wisdom can become a technologically determined "house of certainty." The school and the library, when brought under comprehensive surveillance systems that control against difference, become prisons. To the intellectual and physical constraints Foucault feared, symbolized by the panoptic prison in which a circle of small cells is exposed to a dark guard tower that may or may not be occupied, we have added the presence and participation of automated digital agents.

It was clear to Bacon that new technologies require new visions for their—or, more precisely, our—ends. In Neal Stephenson's novel *The Fall; Or, Dodge in Hell* (2019), the legal will of a brain-dead game-designing billionaire named Dodge commits his family, friends, and fortune to extending his life through technology. They succeed and realize the transhuman dream of digitally extending consciousness into a virtual world. This new "Bitworld" requires humans remaining in "Meatspace," which is falling apart, to reimagine human futures. To support this work, an interdisciplinary research center called the Organization for New Eschatology (ONE) is established. Among their concerns is the role of information, which brings coherence to a world and the identities and relationships embedded in it.

A mysterious character who shows up in a number of Stephenson's books, Enoch Root—whose names link him with the first city in Genesis, immortality, and privileged access to the information system of the universe—wonders if "there are aspects of who we are that will not come back when our brains are scanned and simulated": "It's not clear to me that memory will work, for example, when its physical referents are gone. It's not clear that the brain will know what to do with itself in the absence of a body. Particularly, a body with sensory organs feeding it a coherent picture of the world." Bitworld is a kind of world, but it remains technologically anchored in and intellectually derivative of Meatspace. Dodge's niece Sophia, a principal architect of and agent within Bitworld, says, "To destroy [Bitworld] would *at best* be akin to burning a library. At worst it might be murder." Bitworld has its own libraries: the library is one of the Land's earliest institutions, and it enables Dodge to read his story and recover his identity. And, in a sense, the digitally copied and represented lives that inhabit it are perhaps best understood as living books in a new type of library.

Bacon praised libraries as "shrines" to ancient authors, but also as places for new authors who could develop "more correct impressions, more faithful translations, more profitable glosses, more diligent annotations, and the like." A library is where human intelligence is preserved to be accessed and augmented. After the invention of the library, the library became one of the most important resources and mechanisms for imagining a better world. It provides sources of knowledge, signifies the hope of greater understanding, and provides structures for shaping our engagement with reality. If we were able to create a digital world for our simulated selves, a digital New Atlantis, its nature or ontology would be like that of a digital library. This digital library would be much more than a database: data would be intentionally selected and mediated by both human and artificial agents to facilitate the transformation of data into information, knowledge, and wisdom. This digital New Atlantis would not be a complete or finished world, but a reflection of a much larger and developing world. But a digital library is not entirely digital. At a fundamental level, it depends on physical hardware and infrastructure to sustain it as well as people designing and improving these systems. That primary physical world, inhabited by embodied human agents, would remain more coherent—and interesting. The agency of the libraries and librarians rooted there, hopefully working on the project of something akin to a New Atlantis irreducible to the digital, would be pushing or pulling people toward greater ends.

19 PROMETHEAN HOPES

Mary Shelley is often credited with writing the first modern work of science fiction, *Frankenstein: Or, the Modern Prometheus*, published in 1818. Daisy Hay describes the book as an "assemblage"—a collection of ideas, influences, objects, people, paper, and places—which imagines a possible future arising from the scientific and technological discoveries of the late eighteenth and early nineteenth centuries. Prometheus is the Titan god who stole fire from the gods and gave it to humans, and Shelley's new Prometheus Victor Frankenstein seeks a technique to create new life from dead bodies. Frankenstein succeeds in learning "the secrets of heaven and earth" and creates a living being, but he creates without love and sets in motion a dark creation story. Horrified by his creation, Frankenstein immediately abandons his creature; and all who behold its monstrous appearance flee from it. Formed only by books and rejection, Frankenstein's creature becomes a monster who takes life. Like Satan in the Apocalypse of John, "who aspired to omnipotence" and rebelled against God's paradise, Frankenstein becomes "chained in an eternal hell."

In her introduction to the 1831 edition of *Frankenstein*, Shelley, alluding to the opening chapter of Genesis, writes that "invention ... does not consist in creating out of the void, but out of chaos." Frankenstein's tale of scientific discovery is framed by the narrative of an explorer who, like James Cook in 1776, failed to find a Northwest Passage through the Artic. At the same time in history, water and steam were powering an industrial revolution and raising questions about the potential and peril of new forms of human and technological agency. Shelley's imagination was shaped by new scientific discoveries and technological innovations, and her work can be read as a creative response to the chaos created by that new knowledge.

Shelley also wrote one of the first modern postapocalyptic novels, the *Last Man*, published in 1826. Set in the year of *Frankenstein*'s publication, its narrator discovers prophetic leaves of the Sibyl that contain a record of the last human to survive a global plague in the twenty-first century. After the death of everyone around him, the last man is left to console himself with the books and libraries of the dead, "glowing with imagination and power." His last recorded act is to sail off in a boat with a few books to explore the libraries and cities of the world. "I will not live among the wild scenes of nature, the enemy of all that lives," he says. "I will seek the towns—Rome, capital of the world, the crown of man's achievements. Among its storied streets, hallowed ruins, and stupendous remains of human exertion." To the literary record of humanity, the last man adds his own book, the last book, dedicated "to the illustrious dead."

By the early nineteenth century, it was known that plagues spread through exploration, colonization, and commerce could annihilate vulnerable groups. The journals of George Vancouver, who voyaged into the lower portion of the inland sea that he named after his lieutenant Peter Puget in 1792, are filled with notes about depopulation. Vancouver noted abandoned habitations, "fallen into decay," over-run with weeds and with "several human sculls, and other bones, promiscuously scattered about." He also observed marks from smallpox on many of the Indigenous people he met, noting this "deplorable disease" was common and very fatal among them. Vancouver concluded that, "at no very remote period this country had been far more populous than at present."

By the time she wrote *The Last Man*, Shelley herself had suffered the deaths of children, her husband, and others close to her. She was, in her social context, a postapocalyptic survivor—or, as she put it, "the last relic of a beloved race, my companions extinct before me." Human agency faces an absolute end in *The Last Man*, but human aspirations remain present in the powerful technologies with which they had contended against natural agency. The last man laments:

> Farewell to the giant powers of man—to knowledge that could pilot the deep-drawing bark through the opposing waters of shoreless ocean,—to science that directed the silken balloon thorough the pathless air,—to the power that could put a barrier to mighty waters, and set in motion wheels, and beams, and vast machinery, that could divide rocks of granite or marble, and make the mountains plain.

On the last pages of the last man's book, he announces a final voyage of discovery. The "libraries of the world are thrown open to me—and in any port I can renew my stock" of books, he says. He claims to sail off with "no expectation of alteration for the better." With his imagination failing, the last man is left without any clear hope or joy, or even fear. Yet "restless despair and fierce desire of change" lead him on, suggesting at least a search for new hope.

Shelley translates the last imagined book into a prophetic work for the industrial age. It is an apocalyptic epistle, warning of a natural existential threat that greater human knowledge and agency might address. In *Frankenstein*, Shelley is concerned with the perils of an unrestrained or undisciplined imagination. In *The Last Man*, she seems more concerned with the limits of human intelligence. Frankenstein is more like Prometheus's brother Epimetheus (which could be translated as "afterthought"), who is associated with all the evils released from Pandora's box. What the world of *The Last Man* needed was a true Prometheus (or "forethought"), who could find a technological innovation that could create hope and a new life in a fearful and dying world. The figure of Prometheus is invoked regularly now in connection with AI. Among the mythical lessons associated with the intelligence that came with fire—"the teacher / showing all mankind the way to all the arts there are"—there flows through ancient and modern writers such as Aeschylus and Shelley the call for careful thinking about the future and technology. Forethought, which is resourced richly through books and libraries both real and imagined, helps us to avoid undesirable futures as well as to create more desirable ones.

20 A CANTICLE FOR LIBRARIES

The fall of the Roman Empire in the fifth century created chaos throughout the lands it had touched. According to Walter Scheidel, it also created "conditions that enabled transformative development." Christians, who first suffered under and then gained power through Rome, inhabited imperial cities as well as alternative monastic communities. Libraries were prominent in both, supplying resources for contemplative lives in Edenic gardens and active lives in apocalyptic cities. Post-imperial cities were not only apocalyptic in the revelatory sense, uncovering the declining power of imperial ambitions; they also suffered as targets of aspiring (if doomed) imperialistic ambitions. Remote monasteries, therefore, often served as safer archival sites. Cassiodorus left Rome around 538 to establish a monastery, and an extensive library—including classical literature that supported the study of sacred literature—was at the center of his plan. Because of bookish monks like Cassiodorus, who preserved works that otherwise would have been lost, the medieval library became an image of cultural survival.

Walter Miller updated this image of the monastic library in his postapocalyptic novel *A Canticle for Leibowitz* (1959). After a nuclear "Flame Deluge," enraged survivors destroy what remains of recorded knowledge and technology. Against this "Simplification," Isaac Edward Leibowitz, an engineer-turned-monk, joins a religious order in the American Southwest "to preserve human history" for the descendants of those who desired its destruction. Throughout centuries of cultural darkness, a religious order inspired by Leibowitz keeps a fragmentary record of human knowledge. Even though this information becomes as inscrutable to the monks as it is to the other inhabitants of their illiterate world, the monks preserve its "symbolic structure" with the hope that one day this information will be analyzed, integrated, and restored—reincarnated in a culture—as applied knowledge.

To those outside the Leibowitzian monastery, it seems impossible that there once were humans who invented machines that flew into space, talked, and seemed intelligent. But after twelve centuries of faithfully preserving literacy and learning, the "flame of knowledge" curated by monks is rediscovered. Some knowledge is resurrected, and a period of renaissance begins. A more advanced civilization emerges, but not all the knowledge and experience of the past civilization and its caretakers is learned or improved upon. Knowledge of good and evil grow together and a familiar pattern of self-destruction escalates, culminating in another nuclear war. The order is forced to take its mission of preservation into space, trusting that greater wisdom will, eventually, emerge.

During the Second World War, Miller participated in the destruction of the abbey at Monte Cassino. Benedict established the first house of his order there around 529, but it was sacked and abandoned within fifty years. The abbey was reestablished in the eighth century, sacked and abandoned again in the ninth, and reestablished again in the tenth century. It thrived during the next few centuries, but the peace of the monks continued to be disrupted over the centuries by both natural and human events. The library was built and rebuilt many times, and in some form incredibly survived the depredations of the centuries. Like the Leibowitzian Order, Benedict's sixth-century *Rule*—itself written during civilizational collapse—ordered the work of monks toward seeking truth and doing good in the midst of chaos.

Benedict's *Rule* presumes a whole literary culture of reading and making books, and libraries were necessary for and among the productions of Benedictine monks. Indeed, as the Benedictine monk Jean Leclercq observes, Benedict "takes for granted the existence of a library" in the monastery. In the *Rule*, reading is a prescribed part of daily life, and a number of hours are set aside for this labor. It states that, each year, a monk receives a book from the library "to be read straight through." At the end of the *Rule*, Benedict declares the contents of his text are only the "beginning of monastic life." There are other books to supplement his, and he names several of them. When Giovanni Boccaccio visited the Monte Cassino library in the middle of the fourteenth century, he found "many and diverse volumes of ancient and foreign works." Perhaps envious of the substantial collection of ancient manuscripts humanists such as he sought to obtain, Boccaccio blamed the monks for the sad state of the library without acknowledging the impact a recent earthquake and political turmoil had had on the monastery. Although Boccaccio and book-hunters like him presented the monastic library as a sign of a dark age that was passing, the reality is that libraries such as the one at Monte Cassino provided sources for the European Renaissance.

Monastery libraries exist to provide for temporal as well as eternal ends. They provide monks with books needed for daily study, but this work is expected to "profit [them] forever." This faith for the future leads to hope in and for the present. The library of the Order of Leibowitz resourced the rebirth of civilization, and its curators attempted to point to apocalyptic ends that were not destructive but transformative. Much knowledge had been preserved, but not all this knowledge was good. Monastic libraries that survived the Middle Ages resourced the Renaissance and the expansion of literacy and learning throughout the West. Monasteries, often set up as alternatives to cities in times of chaos, through their libraries became sources of hope for new enlightened cities. The last part of *Canticle* occurs many millennia in the future, but it resembles our late modern age of enlightenment. Apparently absent from Miller's doomed Earth is the presence of other libraries providing additional sources of hope, such as the public ones that fill our present cities. In a brief essay titled "Spreading Enlightenment," San Francisco City Librarian Luis Herrera articulates the enduring hope of these libraries today: "welcoming all who come through its doors ... providing open and free access to information, spreading knowledge and enlightenment, and transforming the lives of its users." Such a statement, echoed by many library advocates, is like a song of praise or canticle for libraries. It is also a canticle for the human spirit.

21 FACING THE END WITH LIBRARIES

In a number of postapocalyptic works, libraries are created or re-created to recover what was lost and to rebuild civilization. For example, in Margaret Atwood's MaddAddam Trilogy—*Oryx and Crake* (2003), *The Year of the Flood* (2009), and *MaddAddam* (2013)—a biological catastrophe results in the collapse of civilization, which is followed by a rebirth of literacy. Before "the flood," the world was a place where people had to be careful about creating "permanent writing" their enemies could find. Also, "the Internet was such a jumble of false and true factoids that no one believed what was on it any more, or else they believed all of it, which amounted to the same thing." Still, writing was needed to think and to communicate wisdom, liturgies, and other practices necessary for survival before and after the flood. After the flood, writing is reintroduced to remember and know again past words, to share knowledge, and to create new stories for a new world. The practices of reading and writing, making ink and paper, and caring for and copying physical books is transmitted to future generations. The ends or goals of libraries may fail before the fall, but they may be recovered after.

Libraries can also help us prepare for a fall. Under the shadow of the rising Third Reich, Isaac Asimov began exploring the rise and fall of empires through a series of stories that began to appear in 1942. Many of these stories were collected into his Foundation Trilogy: *Foundation* (1951), *Foundation and Empire* (1952), and *Second Foundation* (1953). Inspired by Edward Gibbon's *Decline and Fall of the Roman Empire* (1776–89), Asimov imagined a self-satisfied and static Galactic Empire on the brink of collapse. Taking a mathematical approach to social dynamics, "psychohistorian" Hari Seldon calculates that after the fall of the empire there will be a return to feudalism for thirty millennia until another empire emerges. To reduce the projected time needed for recovery, Seldon plans for the establishment of two "foundations." The first is organized at the periphery of the galaxy, with the charge to prepare an "Encyclopedia Galactica." This "giant summary of *all* knowledge" will protect it from being lost, enabling future generation to build on it without having to rediscover it: "One millennium will do the work of thirty thousand." By the time the empire falls, "copies will exist in every major library in the Galaxy." The location and mission of the second foundation remains hidden for centuries.

The first Foundation, focused for decades on preserving the knowledge of the past, begins to suffer from its own inertia. Seldon reveals, through a prerecorded message, that the encyclopedic project was a hoax, meant to divert imperial attention from a much larger plan for "a new and greater Empire." The first Foundation does become a refuge where "art, science, and technology" is incubated for the coming empire, but their knowledge is incomplete and eventually it seeks out the second for help. The search for the Second Foundation leads to the great Imperial Library, alone preserved among the ruins of the empire. There, the plan for the foundations had been created and records about their origin had been deposited. One person, after living for years in the depths of the library, had discovered the secret of the plan but was killed to prevent the secret from being exposed. The secret, hidden in plain sight, was that the Second Foundation was headquartered at the heart of the Galactic Empire, where the plan originated and all its data were kept—in the Library, the beginning, center, and end of everything.

Planning for civilizational collapse also occurs in Neal Stephenson's novel *Seveneves* (2015), which opens with the announcement that, "The moon blew up without warning and for no apparent reason." To escape the coming deluge of fire—the "Hard Rain" caused by the break-up of the moon's remains—the governments of the world collaborate to build a space ark. A high-tech upgraded version of its biblical predecessor, filled with representatives "of every living thing of all flesh," this "Cloud Ark" is intended to preserve select humans and a comprehensive digital repository of Earth's genetic and cultural heritage. This new ark must transcend any "traditional legacy-passing schemes" and preserve humankind and culture for five millennia until a new Earth can be created. The hard news about the end of the old Earth is shared with the world at Crater Lake, Oregon, where natural and human history reveal a prophetic message "for anyone who wanted to read it": "Between six and eight thousand years ago, an unimaginable catastrophe had befallen this place ... surviving humans had kept the story alive in legends of an apocalyptic struggle between the gods of the sky and of the underworld."

The first sign of hope for humanity in *Seveneves* is seen in the responses of those of the last generation of the Age of the One Moon, who collectively engage in their generation's apocalyptic struggle by building out the International Space Station, digitizing everything from genetic sequences to family records, and launching into space as many people and as much stuff as possible. Although only a portion of humanity will survive, everyone is invited to contribute content to "a literary, artistic, and spiritual legacy that would outlive them." And many do transfer their hope in the future to the digital record that will survive them. Five thousand years later, when the biological descendants of seven Eves are ready to return to Earth, those from the sky discover they are not the only ones who have survived. The selections made above, represented in and through the massive digital library in the sky, have terrestrial counterparts below in paper records and living books. New political conflicts emerge over New Earth, but in the final scene a few characters raise questions about "the Agent"—the unknown cause that blew up the moon—and about the purpose of all the struggles they have endured. Such questions are left open, but the fact that humanity survives with libraries is an important image of human hope.

There are real-world projects today to build libraries that could restart civilization. The Long Now Foundation, for example, curates a library collection that constitutes a "Manual For Civilization"—the most essential human knowledge that would help reestablish human culture. Every library, to some extent, functions as a manual for culture. The intention of every library worthy of the descriptor involves the preservation and perpetuation of the cultural goals that created and continue to create it. A real threat to a good future is that not enough of these libraries, which in aggregate represent human culture broadly, will survive to enable humans to thrive in the future. To abandon, destroy, or close a library is to abandon, destroy, and close off future hopes. A library presumes and points toward a future, but it cannot ensure one on its own without constant human attention, care, and commitment.

22 LIBRARY 2041

In *AI 2041: Ten Visions for Our Future*, scientific forecasting and speculative fiction come together to imagine a realistic and hopeful future for AI. Collaborating with AI expert Kai-Fu Lee, the science-fiction writer Chen Qiufan tells ten stories about AI in 2041. At the end of the book, Lee concludes that AI "will open the door to a radiant future for humanity": "AI will create unbelievable wealth, amplify our capabilities through human-AI symbiosis, improve how we work, play, and communicate, liberate us from routine tasks, and ... usher in an age of plentitude." We will "explore what makes us human and what our destiny should be." At the same time, Lee acknowledges, "AI will bring about myriad challenges and perils." But in each *AI 2041* story, he claims, "our sense of justice, our capacity to learn, our audacity to dream, and our faith in human agency always saved the day."

There are no libraries or librarians in *AI 2041*. There are a couple of references to digital archives, but information is not something intentionally curated through knowledge institutions and infrastructures. It seems as though Alexa has thoroughly replaced the dream of its namesake, the Library of Alexandria. Printed books only become important when digital society collapses, which happens in a story titled "Quantum Genocide," and education seems mostly concerned with acquiring skills for whatever jobs remain. In spite of commendable affirmations of humanistic values—"creativity, resourcefulness, tenacity, wisdom, courage, compassion, and love"—the stories in *AI 2041* seem to prioritize AI systems for industrial efficiencies and ends over more human-focused systems, such as libraries, for knowledge creation and augmentation.

At the center of Chen's story "Twin Sparrows," which explores natural language processing and the role of AI in education, two sets of adoptive parents of separated twins debate two worldviews related to AI. One family, thoroughly committed to conventional economic success (their family motto is "Only the best deserve the best"), thinks AI knows best: it can know children better than parents, provide the right information, and it has a "blueprint" for the future. The other family, which identifies as "Homo Tekhne," advocates for a "Technological Artistic Renaissance" that critiques "the blind worship of science and technology": "Through art, Homo Teckhne sought to restore dignity to humanity and revitalize the connection between humanity and nature." From their perspective, "the increasing use of AI in education meant children were trained to become competitive machines." Real education, they believe, should increase "self-awareness through inward exploration, cultivating empathy, communication, and other 'soft skills' that would nurture deeper connections with one another and increase their emotional intelligence"—skills that AI "usually ignored." Each twin struggles within his separate family and their distinct worldview. When the twins are reunited as adults, through AI that had been programmed to keep them connected, they discover they need to combine their views of the world. "AI has shaped us, and we have shaped AI in turn," one twin explains. But the twins "are like two frogs who have each built a well," each seeing "only a small piece of sky." "Perhaps if we connect our wells," he adds, "we will see a bigger world." By combining their AIs and own perspectives, their previous competitive and divided lives open up to "boundless possibilities."

A generative pre-trained transformer, or GPT, is a key AI technology in "Twin Sparrows." Made popular with the release of OpenAI's ChatGPT model in November 2022, a GPT is trained on large datasets to generate probable responses to prompts based on past patterns in the data. When a generative AI model trained on massive corpora of texts is prompted to create new text, in the form of an answer to a question or addressing a topic in a particular genre, the model generates an output by attempting to identify the most relevant parts of texts and predicting probable sequences. According to Lee, these models "exhibit selective memory and attention mechanisms that can selectively remember anything 'important and relevant' in the past." Generative AI outputs are not always helpful or meaningful, though, due to bad data sources and false predictions. Nevertheless, GPTs have convinced some that AI is or soon will be capable of "thinking" and "understanding"—even though this automated statistical processing of data is void of reflective attention on information and deep understanding.

When integrated with good information sources and practices, generative AI models can augment and advance human intelligence in significant ways. Soon after the release of ChatGPT, I used a chatbot built on GPT-3 for the book *Office Shock: Creating Better Futures for Working and Living*. The book, which provides strategies for thinking about the future of office workspaces, is relevant for library spaces but does not address these specifically. But the bookbot was able to make connections and draw conclusions from the book that were similar to ones that I, with some expertise, had found implicit in the text. Since then, I have seen impressive and rapid developments in conversational AI assistants that facilitate accelerated access and enhanced engagement with scholarly literature and research. Beyond mastery of a book or domain of knowledge, however, Lee imagines a future GPT that is an "all-knowing sequence transducer contain[ing] all the accumulated knowledge of human history." It "will read every word ever written and watch every video ever produced and build its own model of the world. ... All you'll have to do is ask it the right questions." Lee does point out problems with current GPTs, which have "absorbed human biases, prejudices, and malice." Rather than extending past patterns, what we most need are models with which we may interact that can help us imagine and create models of better worlds—addressing the errors of the past, facilitating improvements in the present, and planning for better futures. Many ongoing interventions will be required to ensure AI does not replicate, reinforce, and amplify past problems and create a less desirable present and future. And much more human work will need to be done to imagine futures greater than what AI can predict with data. Missing from *AI 2041* is the power of the library to curate good scholarly and cultural resources, cultivate attention and the imagination through engagement with these, and support forms of structural agency that could enable us to leverage AI for beneficial intelligence augmentation and automation. Humans still need to conceptualize and ask the right questions and understand how AI can best participate in helping us create, refine, and answer them. Augmented with AI, libraries can help us create a future enhanced with—rather than inhibited by—artificial agency.

For a recent conference, I was prompted to consider what libraries might be like in 2451—a year alluding to Ray Bradbury's novel *Fahrenheit 451* with its human library project. Some futurists imagine plausible futures by looking backward, to uncover past patterns, and looking to the present for signals of change. The goal with such approaches to futures thinking "is to imagine and make a better future while not remaking old mistakes." Looking backward 426 years, we see a world that had been transformed by the printing press, gunpowder, and the compass. According to Francis Bacon, these technologies significantly impacted knowledge, politics, and exploration. They also elevated the importance and role of libraries in society. In 1599, Thomas Bodley appointed the first Bodleian librarian, as part of his plan to restore Oxford University's library. That same year, the Jesuit educational plan *Ratio Studiorum* was issued, which required annual funding for building up an institution's library. Today, because of plans such as the *Ratio* and librarians and libraries like Bodley's, the library is at the center of current technological and social transformations. When prompted to describe the library in the year 2451, a generative AI model predicted that libraries will be "immersive, dynamic, and ethical hubs for the preservation, exploration, and creation of knowledge across multiple dimensions—physical, virtual, and interstellar." These libraries will "actively shape the evolution of thought, culture, and human (or multi-species) understanding, serving as both protectors of history and incubators of the future." One can be encouraged by this vision, since it is based on training data about what libraries have been and are. And one may be further encouraged, since we can augment this vision with even greater hopes.

23 TRUSTING A FUTURE LIBRARY

Future Library is a 100-year project conceived by the Scottish artist Katie Paterson that is creating a library for the future. This project does not concern a present library that will continue operating in the future, or a library that will open in the near future. The *Future Library* is a library that will become a reality in the next century. Each year the Future Library Trust commissions a new manuscript for the library, which will be preserved in manuscript form until 2114. Until then, only the titles of manuscripts will be revealed. The first manuscript, "Scribbler Moon" by Margaret Atwood, was commissioned in 2014 and additional manuscripts have been solicited from well-known writers from around the world. To provide paper for the library's future books, a forest of one thousand trees was planted in Nordmarka, north of Oslo, Norway. The current plan is for the trees to be made into paper and the manuscripts to become published books, beginning in 2114. But final decisions about the trees and texts will be entrusted to future trustees.

The seeds of this future library—which so far include a few manuscripts and three-foot spruces that will help transform them into paper books—have been planted. The city of Oslo has agreed to protect the manuscripts and the forest over the next one hundred years. In 2022, the Silent Room on the top floor of Oslo's main city library, Deichman Bibliotek, opened to the public. Lined with wood from the Nordmarka forest toward which the room is oriented, this tree-like room has a locked glass drawer for each manuscript. The room provides a small and intimate space where visitors may contemplate this coming library for authors and readers yet unborn. Paterson also encourages people to visit the forest for the library, to "watch the forest grow and change" as "the writers' words [are] forming invisible chapters in the trees."

Margaret Atwood calls *Future Library* a project "immersed in hope." Similarly, David Mitchell, the second author to contribute to *Future*

Library, describes the project as "a vote of confidence in the future." It is also, more fundamentally, an act of trust in those who will shape it. In the notes accompanying his manuscript, Mitchell wrote in 2015: "We have to trust our successors, and their successors, and theirs, to steer the project through a hundred years of political skullduggery, climate change, budget cutbacks and zombie apocalypses … Trust is a force for good in our cynical world, and the *Future Library* is a trust generator." "Ultimately," journalist Richard Foster adds after quoting Mitchell in his coverage of the project, "*Future Library* is an expression of hope—a statement of confidence in the possibilities that could lie ahead for our children over long-term time." Without trust in the social institutions we create to be a force for good in and for the future, we risk losing vital mechanisms for realizing shared hopes.

Future Library represents the practice of long-term thinking, an orientation to the future that enabled our ancestors to conceive and create multigenerational projects. Ancient city structures were the work of generations, and libraries were created to speak to distant generations about the people and stories behind and within them. Today, when massive buildings and technological projects can be completed within a few years—and erased in much less time—neither the past nor the future seems distant. The city of Las Vegas is a sign of such a-temporality. The aspiring high-end Las Vegas I visited in 2021 was very different from the more family-friendly city I visited in 1995, which was altogether different from the rowdy city I experienced in 1980. During the 2020 pandemic, when the casinos closed and turned off their lights, time was suspended for most of the city until business could begin again. Everything depended on the resumption of consumption. Although Las Vegas has a unique and rich history, which can be discovered in local libraries and museums, for most visitors to the city the past and future collapse into a constantly re-created present.

In 1971, disillusioned about the future of his country, Hunter S. Thompson visited Las Vegas and saw in it a reflection of a new dark age in which human promise and potential had been reduced to desperate narcissistic and nihilistic pursuits. Based on two visits—involving two abused convertibles, two trashed hotel rooms, a series of drug-fueled episodes that culminate in two visits to Circus Circus (which he twice calls the "main nerve" of the debased American Dream), and two laments about lost hopes—Thompson rapidly wrote and published *Fear and Loathing in Las Vegas: A Savage Journey to the Heart of the American Dream*. The book is an apocalyptic critique of the dawning commercialized information age characterized by a "loveless monetarism," hidden computers automatically sorting people and optimizing operations, and robot-like people serving extractive mechanisms for predictable and controllable outcomes. As Thompson's political activism before and after this book reveals, fear and loathing had not completely displaced his hope and longing for a better world. Near the end of *Fear and Loathing*, he writes, "The question, as always, is *now* ... ?" The question of whether or not humans may "achieve the freedom and love they imagine to be possible" is literally left open with a question mark. Thompson, the subversive son of a librarian, added this book—and many more—to the library with the hope that others would keep asking and exploring such deep and open questions.

What Thompson failed to see in Las Vegas and in his country—although they were there, if difficult to see—were trustworthy institutions of hope. Trust has continued to decline in public institutions over the last fifty years, but trust in the library as a social institution and infrastructure for good still remains strong. Which itself is a sign of hope. Every library begins, like *Future Library*, with a collective intention to create and mediate a collection or context for discovery for a community. The subsequent histories of libraries preserved important continuities but also changes as they adapted to anticipated as well as unanticipated circumstances. And, as they pointed toward possible and better futures, libraries became signs of human hopes and transformative agents for realizing these. Libraries help us recover from, prepare for, overcome, and even avoid the various challenges we face. If we lose our trust in them, we lose a vital force for human hope and flourishing.

24 THE POSTDIGITAL LIBRARY

In early 2020, with a fellowship from the New York Public Library, Justin Smith was in New York working on a book "that was going to articulate how the internet is destroying the fabric of human community." Suddenly finding himself in lockdown during the COVID-19 pandemic, "cut off from [his] precious books" and the library, Smith admitted that he could not "see the internet as anything other than the force that is holding that fabric together." The book he ended up writing instead, *The Internet Is Not What You Think It Is*, considers the internet in a slightly more positive tone. There are many problems with the internet as it is today, with its commercialization and manipulation of our attention and agency, but Smith acknowledges that some good intentions and elements remain. Smith sees the internet as an attempt to realize the ancient quest to increase and integrate our knowledge of the world. As an example of the potential of the internet to leverage automated and human intelligence, Smith points to and cites Wikipedia. Trapped in his Brooklyn cell, highlighting both its open content and editorial structure, Smith claims Wikipedia

> is the one large-scale internet project that does not seem to be showing the signs of corruption that have become impossible to deny nearly everywhere else in the past decade, the one part that does not seem to have veered off course from the utopian dream that emerged in early modern Europe of machine-assisted learning for the betterment of humankind.

In Wikipedia, Smith glimpses the ambitions of Francis Bacon, Gottfried Wilhelm Leibnitz, and the encyclopedists of the Enlightenment being fulfilled partially. Wikipedia is a community project with "a sincere and non-dogmatic concern to adhere to the truth." Through projects such as

Wikipedia, we can imagine how the internet—when governed by human values and hopes—can enable the creation of new digital platforms for augmenting human intelligence. These are even more powerful when they are integrated into libraries.

The word "digital" often has been used as a proxy for the future, as well as a term for alternatives to past and present things and practices. But digital technologies are no longer new, and digital things are always connected with non-digital things. We began to add a digital dimension to our lives when we began generating, processing, and storing data in the binary digits of 1 and 0 in the mid twentieth century. When these digital data are well structured and meaningful, we describe them as digital information. And, because it is meaningful, digital information is important for our self-understanding and our understanding of the world. Not everything—and certainly not everything meaningful—is reducible to digital data; our reality is a hybrid one. Digital hybridity is a relatively new phenomenon, and we are still reconfiguring our understanding of ourselves and our world, as well as our practices, around it. Hybridity, however, is as ancient as us: we have always been entangled with our technologies.

As digital technologies continue to transform our reality, especially with AI, the challenge of our present information revolution is to imagine what we will be when we become *post*-digital. Increasingly, digital technologies are part of our common lives and the qualifier "digital" is losing its value. This happens with most technologies: print books became books, electric lights became lights, digital computers became computers, and so on. This has already happened with many of the AI applications we use regularly, such as email spam filters, online recommendations systems, and the facial and voice recognition systems we use to interact with our smartphone. Only the newest forms of AI, such as the self-learning models that adapt as we feed them new data, are consistently referred to as AI. But to be postdigital is not simply about living after the time when we no longer need to identify technologies as digital. More fundamentally, being postdigital means assuming critical perspectives about our present engagement with digital technologies—and considering what desirable integrations with digital technologies might look like in the future. The main goal of such reflections, Luciano Floridi says, involves "grasping which questions are, or will be, interesting to ask not only now, but also in the future."

The profound and irrevocable shift we are experiencing as we transition to the postdigital presents many promising and problematic considerations. It forces us to revisit or visit foundational questions about what we can know and how we know it, what we may hope, and what we should do. There has always been too much to know, but the present scale of human and artificially generated information is unprecedented, overwhelming, and prioritizes the immediate experiences of the present. Historically, libraries have attempted to select what was important for their communities to sustain a broad experience of temporality. As information proliferated beyond what one library could contain, libraries established networks to extend access; those networks continue to expand today, through local and global library consortia. Digital materials entered library collections decades ago, and increasingly complex digital objects are now curated by libraries and new consortia. The irony of the abundance of digital information is that everything seems available and permanent, but not everything is available and what is available is impermanent. The digital deluge may be followed by a digital dark age—as bits flip, data are orphaned, websites are abandoned, and corporations die—unless libraries are permitted by content creators to curate digital materials and funded by governments and other institutions to mitigate against technological obsolescence.

Some years ago I heard Tony Ageh, then Chief Digital Officer at the New York Public Library, describe the four major challenges facing the digital transformation of libraries. He called these "the four agents of the digital apocalypse," alluding to the four riders bringing world-ending forces in the Apocalypse of John. He named them obsolescence, mass surveillance, obfuscation or lack of transparency, and ambivalence—or, more precisely, apathy. The last apocalyptic agent, apathy, is the most dangerous. Apathy, not distraction, is the opposite of attention. As James Williams points out, the design of many digital technologies interferes with our attention at many levels. If we are distracted from doing the tasks we want to do, we are distracted from becoming who we want to be. And if we are distracted from the things we care about, we may lose fundamental capacities, such as reflection and intelligence, which enable us to define these. Without attention, we may trade information—and its potential for transformation—for deformation. Through both selection and mediation, the library has been, is, and will continue to be an institution designed for informing and forming human cares.

The "digital" encompasses software and hardware, private and public organizations, designers and users, and laws and practices. It also includes, assembled through these, increasingly autonomous agents that can operate, develop, and discover information independent of us. Libraries participate in the ecosystem that connects all these entities, and they should have leading integrative roles in shaping our emerging postdigital environment. These roles are both conserving and liberating. In addition to collecting and preserving digital resources, libraries and librarians help people learn digital literacies, overcome digital naïveté, and enable digital participation. Beyond technological competencies, libraries provide resources, services, and spaces for critical and ethical reflection on—as well as constructive engagement with—the digital transformation of our lives and world. Floridi identifies four tasks in an ethical approach to the design and governance of the digital: critical awareness of problems, signaling that they matter, engaging with affected stakeholders, and designing and implementing shared solutions. Libraries can participate in and facilitate engagement in each of these tasks, supporting Floridi's call for ethics to "inform strategies for the development and use of digital technologies from the beginning, when changing the course of action is easier and less costly in terms of resources, impact, and missed opportunities." As sources, signs, and structures of hope, libraries can transform our imagination about what is possible with and beyond the digital as we seek to integrate new technologies into our lives in ways that help us realize a better and more just world.

PART FOUR

THE LIBRARY AS A PLACE OF ACTION: HOW LIBRARIES ARE STRUCTURES FOR HOPE

H   Social Sciences
J   Political Science
L   Education
Q   Science
T   Technology

25 THE LIBRARY AT DAWN

One of the pleasures and prerogatives of running a library is being in the building, ahead of the dawn, before the doors are opened to others who wish to begin their day in the library. Some libraries come to life slowly, others quickly. But there is always the promise that life will fill the library in both expected and unexpected ways. In the medieval liturgy of the hours, Vigils marks a time between night and day—echoing the moment, unwitnessed by any human—when some traditions believe Christ rose from the dead. For nearly a millennium and a half, between the middle of the night and the dawn of day, monks have risen from the dead of night to wait and hope for a new day of life. Praying words as if from the tomb, monks ask for their lips to be opened as light begins to overtake the darkness.

With digitally and globally networked resources, always available to both human and artificial agents, a dimension of the library is always open. But most of our buildings do close, and our digital spaces are largely unpopulated at night by humans. I once worked in a library that never closed while classes were in session. The idea, which came from the college president and not the college librarian, had more to do with marketing than with student success. The idea of never closing a staffed library seemed innovative, and there was an opportunity to be the first to implement it. When the college's library building was renovated and expanded for a second time, at the beginning of this century, a new and spacious reading room was added to the complex. The plan for the room was inspired by the design of late-nineteenth-century reading rooms: bookshelves set in wood-paneled walls, rows of broad wood tables, traditional armchairs and sofas, and a fireplace. The room was also imagined as a site for all-nighters.

Many students loved the idea of a library that was always open, even if the building usually was empty by 2 a.m. Soon after the renovated building opened, some clever students started a challenge in which the last person left studying in the library's new grand reading room would be permitted to enter their reflections in a Moleskine journal kept on the fireplace mantel. Winners were encouraged to record their names, departure times, responsible professors and courses, and the motivations behind their victories. An additional instruction, added a few years into the challenge, was to record "any evidence of notable insanity." After the first journal was full of entries, each year library staff began placing new journals on the mantel and old journals in the archives. Entries in the journals during the first seven years seem mostly sane. Many are silly, some are serious, and a few are sad. The average winning time was around 5 a.m. For the most part, student reflections are full of weariness and regrets about the quality of their work and their use of time.

Initially, I thought the idea of a library building that was always open was a good idea. I loathed the alarms that intruded upon my late-night study sessions in the subterranean depths of Princeton's Firestone Library. (Often I dreamed—in both good and bad dreams—of being locked inside.) I also hated discovering at too late or early an hour a book to which I believed I needed immediate access. Over time, though, I learned that unfinished work could wait or remain unfinished, and that complete knowledge or understanding is never just one book away. I also came to realize that the always-open library building violated a fundamental value of libraries. Unlike the seemingly endless internet, automatically connecting artificial agents that never rest, the library is scaled for human minds and actions. The library is about time and limits, not eternity or infinitude. A library manages information and intellectual overload by providing interfaces and infrastructures that acknowledge and respect human limits. These include catalogs, classification and organization systems, and appropriate furniture and equipment. A library also provides access to librarians, who are ready to help with advisory, reference, research, and other consultative library services when called upon. Human limits are neither uniform nor fixed: different people are productive at different times and in different ways, and we are always finding good ways to extend our abilities and lifespans with technologies. But our brains and bodies impose certain and even absolute constraints on us, which require us to observe regular patterns of rest and sleep. Without sleep, we cannot hold together our mental models of reality. The reading room challenge journals document students' weary recognitions of this.

Another benefit of working in a library is seeing it, day after day, filled with people quietly—usually, but not always—at work individually and with others. In periods without disruption during the day, they are free to think and read, dream and nap, listen and learn, watch and pray, and focus on whatever hidden work to which they are giving their attention. This work may be inspired or boring, involve constructive or deconstructive critiques, cause joy or perplexity. Most of this work requires perseverance and hopes for certain outcomes. Much of it will not be revelatory; some of it will be very revolutionary. In defense of the idea of free public library space, Anne Lamott speaks about how revolutionary the notion of access can be. An open library provides "a place where the poor, the marginalized, and the young can find out who they are." If you "cut people off from essential sources of information—mythical, practical, linguistic, political—you break them." You also cut them off from resources for hope. And that is something we and our world always need, perhaps especially now. The library is a unique place where we can cultivate important practices of close reading, writing, and thinking as well as new and more distant forms of these practices with AI.

The liturgy of the hours concludes with Compline, prayers for the completion of the day. As the night arrives, and we enter it defenseless, the final words of the day are for protection and preservation as we prepare for death-like sleep. As important as libraries are for life, a life lived only or too much in a library would be a rather reduced life. The ritual of closing time is not only for the sake of employed library workers. When we make our closing announcements and ring the closing bell, we are calling and sending people into the world—often into the night and darkness, where it is harder to read—directing their attention toward other spheres of life and their agency toward rest. As we rest, we may imagine with Dylan Thomas the congress of millions of words, "each of which was alive forever in its own delight and glory and oddity and light." At night, in the closed library with its own agency, the library sustains memory and hope while awaiting the return of our attention.

26 THE ARCHIVAL CYCLE

Archivists James O'Toole and Richard Cox point out that in ancient Latin *recordare* means to give something "back to the heart and the mind after the passage of time." From this word came the English word "record," which first meant an oral testament and later came to refer to a written document. The etymological and conceptual shift from oral to written records—captured, for example, when Herodotus inscribed oral sources into his histories as testimony—led to what Paul Ricoeur called "the birth of the archive," that "physical place that shelters the destiny of ... the documentary trace." Records and books are among our oldest artifacts. They are also the commonest: there are more cuneiform tablets than ancient palaces; more Greek and Roman inscriptions than temples; and more medieval manuscripts than cathedrals. Now, there are too many digital records to count, and with the proliferation of automatically generated records, there will soon be more records than almost anything else. Changes in the nature and extent of our cultural records are causing us to continue reconceptualizing and reconstituting libraries and archives to support the creation and curation of our cultural record.

The history of archives and libraries is a history of changing communication technologies: from orality to literacy (beginning about six thousand years ago); from scroll to codex (beginning about two thousand years ago); from manuscript to print (beginning about five hundred years ago); and from paper to electronic media (beginning over one hundred years ago). It is important to remember that the current forms and functions of archives, libraries, and similar institutions—and present perceptions of them—were, for the most part, shaped relatively recently. Distinctions between archival and literary documents, in particular, were not clear in antiquity or the Middle Ages. According to Randall Jimerson, the printing press, capable of reproducing texts quickly, helped divide documents into forms "directed toward a mass audience" and others "grounded in personal interactions and organizational transactions." Professionalization of those who worked with such documents began to emerge in the late nineteenth and early twentieth centuries: the American Library Association was organized in 1876; the American Association of Museums in 1906; and the Society of American Archivists in 1936.

Libraries and archives can be positioned within various information lifecycle models. The book lifecycle (see Figure 26.1), a model developed by two bibliographers, identifies "five events in the life of the book": publishing ("the initial decision to multiply a text or image for distribution"), manufacturing, distribution, reception, and survival. In this model, libraries, focusing primarily on the products of print culture, are situated as secondary distributors. Libraries also have had important roles in reception and survival, but the reception role is usually a passive one and survival often has been dependent on such factors as physical form, number of copies, popularity, and where books rested (e.g., on library bookshelves).

The records lifecycle (see Figure 26.2), the classic textbook model for records management, identifies five stages in the life of a record: creation,

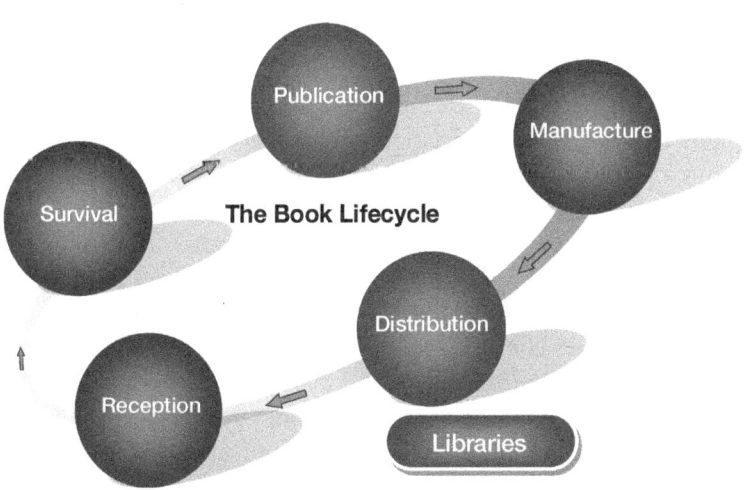

FIGURE 26.1 The Book Lifecycle. Diagram by the author

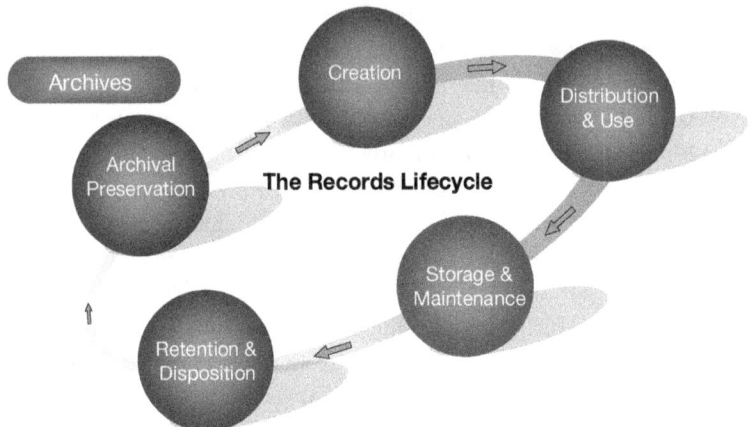

FIGURE 26.2 The Records Lifecycle. Diagram by the author

distribution and use, storage and maintenance, retention and disposition, and archival preservation. Within this model, archives, focusing primarily on unpublished papers, are situated at the end of the cycle, waiting to receive selected or saved records—or, to appropriate Francis Bacon's definition of antiquities, "some remnants of history which have casually escaped the shipwreck of time." Use, both immediate and future, is the cause of these cycles and their continuing iterations.

These two lifecycle models can be merged into an archival cycle (see Figure 26.3), which represents the five major stages in the lives of books and records, however these information artifacts are defined: creation (including human intentions or artificially initiated processes to publish, as well as the technologies of production), distribution (including the process of publication), reception, storage, and preservation (which encompasses selection and survival). In this model, the more traditional situation of most libraries and archives can be plotted. During the twentieth century, libraries collected mostly published books and journals, which were used, saved, and then more things were created to collect. At the same time, archives collected and saved more private records, which were used, and records proliferated. With the proliferation of digital materials, widely dispersed and largely un-curated, the previously established positions of libraries and archives within the archival cycle

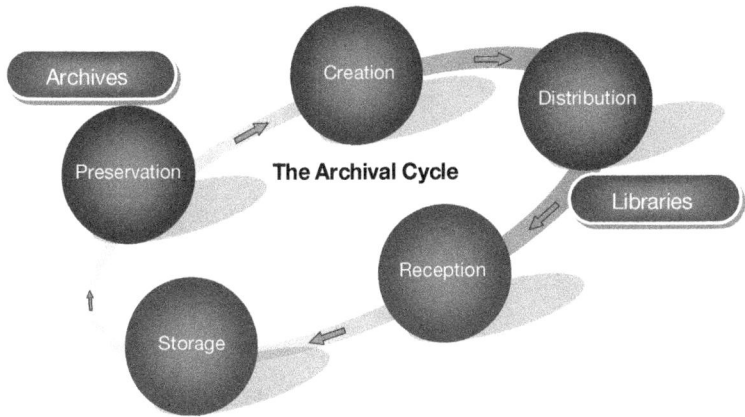

FIGURE 26.3 The Archival Cycle. Diagram by the author

proved problematic. Physical storage media need to be preserved, to maintain the integrity of the bits that reside on them, and the logical ordering of the bits needs to be preserved to ensure they are renderable and readable in the future. There are also larger and more basic questions of responsibility: who will save what, when, how, and where? Common computer applications and uses do not do much to support long-term access, which means digital materials are at risk of being lost if they are not proactively curated.

But libraries and archives have not remained stationary within the archival cycle. Changes in communication technologies and practices have caused libraries to broaden their collecting and distribution activities. Often connected with digital archiving or institutional repository services, for some time libraries have been collecting new types of digital materials, often institutional, including unpublished works, research data, administrative records, local cultural materials, and software. Moving away from a focus on collecting certain types of fixed and final works, libraries became more interested in the process of communication and have been involved in developing new models of communication and publishing services to support authors and editors. Archives, no longer expecting to be able to salvage digital records long after their creation, have become more proactive in the records-creations process. Concern for the creation, dissemination, and preservation of digital materials has led toward a necessary

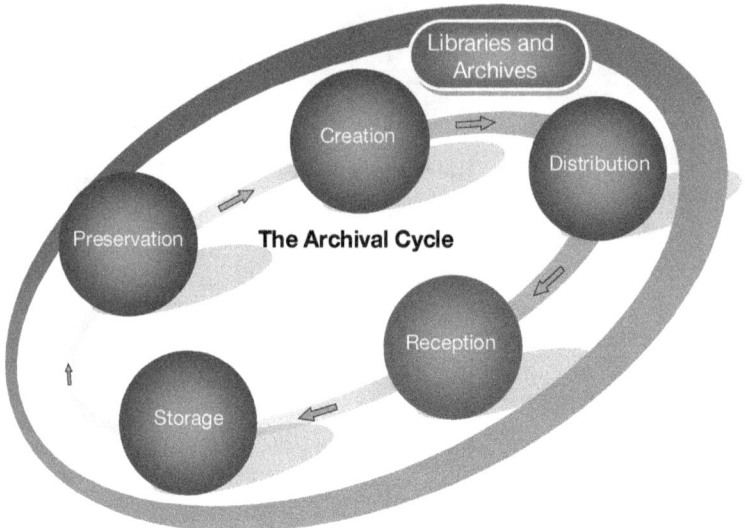

FIGURE 26.4 The Archival Cycle. Diagram by the author

(re)convergence of the missions of libraries and archives to ensure better access to the cultural record—both immediately, through distribution, and over the long-term, through preservation. To fulfill their shared mission, librarians and archivists continue to reposition their institutions within the archival cycle and move closer to the point of creation, where they are able to influence, guide, and control the management of digital materials (see Figure 26.4). AI is already embedded within every stage of the archival cycle—creating and selecting, disseminating and publishing, searching and synthesizing, analyzing and archiving. The next shift is for libraries and archives to ensure that new AI enhancements and dependencies are well designed and audited to sustain the archival cycle.

27 THE FUTURE OF THE BOOK

On the exterior wall of the Archibald S. Alexander Library at Rutgers University, facing the library school I attended, there is a quote from the fourteenth-century English bishop and bibliophile Richard de Bury:

> All the glory of the world would be buried
> in oblivion unless God had provided
> mortals with the remedy of books.

For centuries, the book has been the primary means and metaphor for transmitting information. Now, screens have eclipsed the book as both the means and metaphor for information. Are our screens, or at least some of them, books? Is a book just the device that conveys a message through the symbolic representation of a language? The seventeenth-century Spanish printer Alonso Víctor de Paredes said that a book, like a human being, has a dual nature: it consists of both a soul and a body. But the soul of a book cannot exist without a body, and the body of a book without a soul is an empty container. If we are able to read about the glories of the world throughout its duration, it is because messages about them—*and* the material forms that contain and carry these messages—have been kept from being buried in oblivion.

Books have assumed many material forms over the millennia. For the last five hundred years or so, since the advent and advance of the printing press, the working—but imperfect—definition of a book has been: a long text, printed on sheets of paper bound (or glued) together on one side and placed between covers, and meant for public consumption. But before the eventual hegemony of paper and print, a book was a bound collection of vellum leaves covered with manuscript text. Before the use of the codex to collect such leaves, there were scrolls containing single or multiple book-length texts. The Pentateuch, or the five books of Moses, still may be found in single large scrolls. And before scrolls, texts were inscribed on tablets and the content of a "book" might cover dozens of these, as with the Epic of Gilgamesh. Other materials have and will be used for books: tree leaves, wood, audio formats, digital displays, electronic paper, and virtual environments. Each form affords a different encounter with a book, and different reading practices accompany each form. But the idea of a book—a substantial message, presented through a material medium, to be mediated to readers—has persisted as an essential product of human culture since the information revolution that created information artifacts.

To read a book is to inhabit two worlds simultaneously. A book invites a reader into another world. However congruent the world of the book may be with a reader's world, the abstract world of words exists to become incarnate in the world of the flesh through the reader. The reader never fully escapes the world as it was before an encounter with a book: the seated body is anchored in a fixed time and place, and the demands of the pre-book world and its environment will inevitably reassert certain claims on the mind that temporarily transcends it. As the mind turns its attention away from the abstract environment of a book, it will bring something new into the embodied world. Books enable information to become matter and energy, and as such they shape the present as well as the future. This experience of deep reading is very different from how AI processes the text of a book, and from our distant reading of books summarized by AI. Deep reading—like deep writing and thinking—is a hard-won achievement of humanity, the result of a very long evolutionary and developmental process. Losing it, by entirely outsourcing engagement with complex texts, would diminish us as a species significantly.

To read a book is also to connect with other books. Books are not discrete objects existing independently from other books: they commune with other books, blur into other books, and generate new books. Within the container of a particular book, the contents are more than the central text: there are introductions, indices, and other information that concern the core content. In addition to these "peritexts" that surround the main text, there are "epitexts": texts beyond book, such as reviews and critical analyses published elsewhere, which engage with it. These two types of paratexts connect the substance of a book with a textual community that transcends a seemingly isolated and finite book. The existence of a book invokes and involves participation in a textual community.

In a library, these intertextual relationships are sustained, amplified, and connect with people. Anna-Sophie Springer, in an essay on the importance of the library as a curatorial space, quotes Ray Bradbury who began his literary career working in public libraries. Bradbury, who in *Fahrenheit 451* imagined a diminished world without libraries, observed, "The library was a special, embryonic place where a person could sit with the vibrations of lives off the walls, all around him." Springer also quotes Michel Foucault, who says: "The imaginary is not formed in opposition to reality as its denial or compensation; it grows among signs, from book to book, in the interstice of repetition and commentaries; it is born and takes shape in the interval between books. It is a phenomenon of the library." Libraries are often thought of as simple storehouses of books. Even if that image were true—ignoring the conversations and communities libraries cultivate, among the living and the dead—that dead image would be sufficient to reveal that books and libraries transcend themselves and become something more dynamic and synergistic than their constituent elements. But more significantly, the "interval between books," generated in and through libraries, transforms how we imagine and live in the world.

A book, in essence, could be described as a technology that facilitates reflective attention in connection with a substantial idea. Books are not the only information artifacts that do so, but they remain paradigmatic of the possibility. The contents and forms of books have varied over time; the difference between what is and is not a book is lost somewhere between a technical explanation and a poetic expression. Libraries are those institutions that, concerned with both the technical reality and the poetic possibilities, enable books and other information artifacts to be and do what they are intended to do—or programmed to do, since we are now introducing AI into our authorial community. Libraries do this at scale and through structures that are important for individuals as well as societies, and with the hope that communities of books and readers will continue to grow and perpetuate themselves. As de Bury said, "All things are corrupted and decay in time." Without libraries, many of the glories of the world indeed would be lost in oblivion.

28 THE NEW MEDIA LIBRARY

Before the nineteenth century, the main recording technologies in the West were ink, handmade paper, and the manually operated printing press. As the century progressed, new industrial machines quickly automated papermaking and printing, which led to a proliferation of cheaper printed media. At the same time, communication was being accelerated in time and across space through the telegraph and the railroad. And new communication media began to appear: an image of a Paris street was captured by daguerreotype in 1839; the human voice was captured in an audio recording in 1860. During the first half of the twentieth century, as visual and audial recordings became more accessible, new synchronous media formats became popular: moving pictures in the 1910s, radio broadcasts in the 1920s, and television programming in the 1950s. By the time electronic computers and documents were added to the media mix during the latter half of the twentieth century, print—although still prolific—had lost its dominance within the information environment.

New information and communication technologies require renewed and new institutions, as well as social and technological infrastructures, to reconfigure access to and trust in information. Older information institutions, such as libraries, have always had to adapt to new sources and means of accessing information. In addition to creating more space for printed materials during the twentieth century, libraries had to collect and mediate access to new media. These included publications of old and new material in microformats—which required acquiring sheets and rolls of film, cabinets for storage, and machines for viewing—as well as other photographic and phonographic media in which communities were interested. The public library I grew up with during the latter quarter of the twentieth century provided access to microfiche and microfilms, vinyl records and audio CDs, reel films and VHS cassettes, electronic documents and online databases, and more—as well as printed books, journals, and newspapers. Every library I have worked in has an unofficial collection of various technologies needed for accessing the variety of media formats that have proliferated over the last two hundred years.

Today, digital is the dominant media format and the primary focus of libraries' collecting and mediating activities. Nearly every information resource created today is digital, whether textual, visual, or audial. Even those materials that are given a subsequent physical form, such as printed books, first exist as digitally composed and edited objects. While many still prefer the affordances of print over digital books, the distribution and access advantages of digital books is eclipsing the benefits of print. A digital book can be published and accessible immediately when it is ready for distribution, whereas printing requires additional resources, logistics, and time. Also, a digital book can be searched, copied, and linked with other digital resources in ways that printed books cannot be (at least not presently). Digital books are still in their infancy, though. Like early printed books designed to look like manuscript books, the design of digital books currently depends too much on printed books. In the near future, it is likely that digital books will look different and have additional affordances that enhance readers' engagements with texts. These encounters likely will include artificial agents, like the AI tutor and mentor integrated into *A Young Lady's Illustrated Primer* in Neal Stephenson's 1995 novel *The Diamond Age*.

In her book on developing new digital reading practices, Jenae Cohn highlights three "repeated themes of anxiety" that have accompanied the arrival of new information media: memory loss, pseudo information, and information overload. Cohn points out that we have adapted our information practices to address these anxieties over time, and consequently our practices have become more sophisticated. We remember and know about Socrates' concerns that reading and writing technologies would replace the need for memory, as well as the exchange of information that happened through oral transmission, through Plato's texts and ongoing classroom discussions of them. To contend with the quantity and quality of books produced after the advent of the printing press, the modern research university was organized to shape academic disciplines and disciplined scholars. And, as libraries became the "epicenters of scholarly discovery," librarianship emerged as a profession to help "manage, understand, and keep track of information." We learned to read and take advantage of the distinctive tactile affordances of printed materials—with pencils in hand and fingers between pages—and we will learn to read digital materials better and benefit from their distinct advantages as well.

Digital media present unique challenges to immediate and long-term access. Most current business models for digital resources often inhibit both; they are not aligned entirely with the goals of libraries to provide and preserve broad access. Libraries typically rent rather than own digital content, and contracts restrict access in various ways—for example, to certain users and a certain number of users. Some important open access resources are created and curated by libraries and other institutions, but most digital content is owned by media companies that prioritize profit over access. In addition to the high and rising costs of accessing current digital content, there are open questions about who will ensure future access and how. In the past, when content was no longer profitable but ownership rights had not yet expired, content was often abandoned or, when ownership was not clear, "orphaned." Copyright and patent terms have expanded over time—but they are not perpetual. At some point, they enter the public domain and may be copied or digitized and used in new works without restrictions. But if there is no commercial interest in keeping content available, it enters a space of limited sharing and preservation options. Many physical information artifacts can survive through benign neglect, within or even outside of library buildings. But digital materials, because of their dependencies on technologies that are proprietary and will become obsolete, require more proactive measures, such as updating or migrating to new formats. Without such interventions, digital materials—which constitute most of our cultural record today—will be lost. Moreover, how digital content can and may be used by AI, which could enhance access or further constrain it, involves many open legal and technical questions.

The increasing quantity of new media—especially digital resources, including artificially generated content—elevates the importance of the library's work of selection. Not everything is worthy of attention, now or in the future. In an age of intelligence automation, when artificial agents can process and discover patterns in big datasets, the human advantage will continue to be in finding meaning in smaller and surprising patterns. Both human and artificial intelligence need long-term access to good data. Luciano Floridi reminds us that, "Memory is not just a question of storage and efficient management; it is also a matter of careful curation of significant differences." Looking beneath and beyond the noise of our present digital and automated information environment, libraries can select and mediate access to the good and distinctive digital resources that are most important for their communities—for their needs and hopes, both now and in the future.

29 LIBRARY AUTOMATION AND INTELLIGENCE AUGMENTATION

Libraries were early entrants into the age of automated information processing. Following industrial methods and technologies, library operations—and the buildings that housed them—became more standardized and efficient in the late nineteenth and early twentieth centuries. At the same time, the foundations for the computer revolution were being laid. As librarians were typing bibliographic information onto catalog cards to file in cabinet drawers, other human information processors were punching patterns into cards that could be sorted automatically by tabulating machines. By the 1950s, when the Library of Congress catalog had nearly ten million cards crammed into more than ten thousand drawers, magnetic tapes began to replace punched cards. In 1965, the Library of Congress hired mathematician Henriette Avram to create the first automated cataloging system: Machine-Readable Cataloging (MARC). The first public computer for searching MARC records was installed in the Library's Main Reading Room by 1976, and on December 31, 1980, the last new cards were filed in the Reading Room's card catalog.

It was clear to most librarians by 1970 that libraries were part of a new information environment. This environment had new needs, media, and means of access, all of which were decentering the library in the information exchange process. Surveying the prospects for libraries, a US federal commission reported in 1969 that the greatest technological opportunity for libraries was to automate technical library operations: cataloging, acquisitions, serials control, and circulation. Additional opportunities included online networks and collaborations, distribution of "nonbook" materials, and new user services. New technologies are often used, first, to do old things more efficiently. And, as the commission reported and recommended, the automation of technical operations was the first focus for most libraries. In the 1970s, through collaborative consortia and networked computers, libraries developed automated processes for information exchange.

Libraries began to advance to the next stage of technological innovation in the 1980s: doing new things. With commercial library systems, online public catalogs, public computers, and online searching of remote databases, libraries offered new automated user services as well as new public information services. In the 1990s, libraries consolidated many automated solutions and supported end-user computing as well as internet and database access. By the end of twentieth century, libraries held multimedia collections and provided online access to local as well as global resources—and they were empowering people to search for, use, and create information in new ways. Through all these changes, libraries demonstrated their understanding that material technologies—such as information artifacts, in various forms, and increasingly powerful information access systems—need accompanying formative practices to empower human agency.

In the 1970s, the concept of information literacy was introduced to identify the competencies needed to form people who could navigate a new information environment connected with automated information processing. Building on an earlier notion of bibliographic instruction, information literacy involves identifying information needs and then being able to find, evaluate, and use information to fulfill those needs. Over the last twenty years, as digital resources, services, and spaces have become thoroughly integrated into most libraries, librarians' approaches to information and technological literacies have come to include other literacies. These include data literacy, which involves accessing, assessing, interpreting, using, and managing data, as well as media and digital literacies, which involve the critical use of different information and communication technologies. Most recently, librarians have been exploring the relationship between information literacy and ethics and AI literacy and ethics. At its best, instruction in information and related literacies cultivates the reflective, critical, and responsible use of information.

As automation and intelligent technologies improve, there may be additional opportunities to automate more library services currently performed by humans. But this will require proactive and ethical design, as well as ongoing oversight, to ensure that automation enhances and does not inhibit human creativity, relationships, and ambitions. A recommendation system may assist with discovery and research, but it also might prematurely close off alternative sources of information or promote more popular over more relevant sources. A chatbot may be helpful for providing some basic answers to questions or helping one formulate better questions, but this syntactic processing of information is rather different from the dynamic semantic understanding that happens in humans and in conversations between them. In addition, by distancing people from direct encounters with information resources and systems, AI could decrease our engagement with and understanding of information. Ralph Parker, an early advocate for library automation, cautioned in 1964 that, "there is a danger that the machine will become temporarily the nominal master. Machines have limitations in their capabilities, and the people who operate them tend to let the machine dictate what and how things are done. When this happens, it is a defeat for human ingenuity."

Following the invention of electronic digital computers in the 1940s, leading mathematicians and engineers began working on AI. At the same time, other computer scientists were working on a different project: intelligence augmentation. Instead of trying to simulate human intelligence, they worked on technologies that would help humans do intellectual work such as the personal computer and computer networking. Automated and autonomous information processing technologies challenge human limits: our autonomy from them, our attention independent of them, and our agency beyond them. But, like every other useful technology, they also can help us transcend our limits. Some librarians say libraries are "on the cusp" of a dramatic change connected with AI, and many are hopeful that libraries can adopt and adapt AI technologies and literacies to advance their profession's millennia-long history of augmenting human knowledge and intelligence through new information technologies and practices.

30 FROM ALEXANDRIA TO ALEXA—AND BACK

In the mansion library at Bletchley Park, plans were implemented that began what was, in a way, the first war of intelligent machines. To combat the German Enigma encryption machine, more sophisticated information processing machines were developed at Bletchley for codebreaking that helped end the war on the continent. After the war, many of those who had worked with automated information processing technologies before and during the war continued to focus on creating machines that could simulate human intelligence—launching efforts to create artificial intelligence. Today, sophisticated AI systems can perceive the world through sensors, make decisions using models that represent the world, and "learn" or respond to new data about the world. Present AI technology stacks—which have many limitations and require many human interventions before, during, and after they are deployed— enable AI systems to perform complex tasks that previously required human intelligence. But this complex automated information processing only superficially resembles human decision-making and action, about which our current understanding is still limited, and the development of better AI systems currently is hindered by such issues as data quality, opaque models, incomplete or inaccurate representations of the world, and concerns about adverse social and environmental impacts. We need to understand both the possibilities and problems with AI, and engage with these technologies to improve them.

There was once a library in one of Jeff Bezos's homes, with two fireplaces facing each other from opposite sides of the room. Over one he had inscribed the word "Dreamers," and books by dreamers surrounded it. Over the other, he had inscribed the word "Builders" and it was surrounded by their books. Bezos believes human creativity needs both. Dreamers inspire, and then builders create and enable further inspiration. Amazon's AI assistant Alexa is an impressive technology created in the creative space symbolized by the arrangement of Bezos's library. Inspired by the *Star Trek* computer, in 2011 Bezos pressed his team to create a "device with its brain in the cloud" completely controlled by voice. In 2014, with a rather modest press release, Amazon announced the availability of a voice-activated device called Echo and controlled by the digital assistant Alexa. This technology was not presented as a fully conversational computer, but as a device capable of performing and communicating about some discrete tasks in response to vocal prompts. The product launch was followed by rapid adoption and development, and Alexa became a primary information processing interface in the daily lives of many.

Alexa's name, or "wake word," is an homage to the legendary Library of Alexandria. Like a library, Alexa is an interface for accessing and engaging with information. But libraries, from Alexandria to every local public library today, are much more complex interfaces. Shaped primarily by humans intentionally selecting and mediating information, libraries exist to help people accomplish specific tasks by cultivating their attention and agency. Even as libraries have increasingly automated operations, including with AI, there remains a priority for human intellectual freedom and human interactions that is informed by community and professional values. A proper library, with such deep commitments to human values, provides a well-resourced and generative space where dreamers, builders, and others—living and dead—can come together to imagine and work for a better future. The role of an artificial agent such as Alexa, an assemblage of AI applications interacting with other globally networked AI applications, is more powerful and helpful when it is situated within broader frameworks that prioritize human values and goals.

Libraries and librarians are qualified in unique ways to be direct participants in shaping our AI ecosystem. From the beginning, libraries have been human interfaces for accessing the proliferating variety and volume of information artifacts. Managing the asymmetry between what a human can process and the amount of information available is an ancient problem; as it says at the end of Ecclesiastes, "Of making many books there is no end." Libraries began with the goal of defining and providing a centered, although not strictly bounded, context for discovery. This idea of a selected collection remains helpful. So, too, does the idea of mediating access to a defined discovery domain. Often this access is mediated through librarians, but libraries also provide human-scaled information infrastructures that enable unmediated and automated access that is more equitable than other options. These access systems have included manuscript, printed, and digital catalogs, as well as the classification and organization of materials in physical and virtual spaces. AI technologies already permeate library systems and practices, and new applications are proliferating rapidly for discovery and engagement. As with all library technologies, the goal is to connect people with the information they need or desire and empower them to use it. While digitally networked resources and services have been important augments for libraries, one clear distinction between the library and the internet, accessed through search engines and chatbots, is the lack of human-scaled selection and human-focused mediation.

Prioritizing people requires an acknowledgment of and attention to human limits—not just of our knowledge, but of our existence and dependencies in space and time. We are embodied, even when we are online, and our physical conditions constrain our abilities and ambitions to be omniscient, omnipresent, and omnipotent. Large-scale search engines, large language models, and other technologies can tempt us into thinking we may transcend our attentional and agentic limits thoroughly. But these commercial tools and systems often do not respect the protections that the vulnerabilities of human existence require: personal data protection, humane software design, non-manipulative algorithms, and space for reflection and inspiration. These systems do not help us explore fully hopes that actually may enable us to transcend ourselves; such hopes are beyond the limits of their programming. Libraries' long history of designing human-centered physical and digital information infrastructures and services can be a model for AI alternatives that respect human limits and diverse needs.

Educators José Antonio Bowen and C. Edward Watson point out that "AI is becoming a new, powerful partner" that will change how we think and work. AI can help us "clarify [our] thoughts, explore new ideas, increase divergent thinking, and perhaps even become more creative." Libraries are in a unique position to educate and equip people to understand and use AI well, including preparing all of us for the future of work with AI—not as passive users but as active participants in shaping the future. The general-purpose nature and extensive presence of AI in our lives means that this technology must be developed with wisdom drawn from many sources. Better understanding and applications of AI require much more than technological expertise; good AI will be shaped by diverse perspectives, global conversations, regulatory frameworks, and collective action. To increase awareness of AI and its impacts, libraries can provide resources and instruction, and facilitate community conversations that are open and inclusive. By supporting career exploration and vocational discernment, teaching transdisciplinary AI competencies, and cultivating ethical reflection on the role of AI in work and life, libraries can empower people to find meaningful and appropriate ways of engaging with AI. Such strategies will enable people to participate within their own domains of influence—whether they are designers, influencers, regulators, or users of AI—which will broaden and diversify how we adopt and adapt AI collectively, but also contextually. As people learn more about AI, they are likely to become more ambivalent about it, seeing that the great potential of these technologies is mixed with significant challenges. For example, Alexa depends on a commercial model of mass surveillance that is foreign to libraries, which prioritize individual privacy rights and implement systems that preserve freedom from surveillance. Libraries have a unique opportunity to guide the development of AI as well as our engagement with it, and to collaborate with other efforts to create better technologies with more clarity, caution, care, and creativity.

31 THE LIBRARY AND VIRTUE

Libraries are shaped by—but also have a critical role in shaping—shared values, goals, and hopes related to information. People who work in libraries help individuals and societies discern meaning amid all the data they encounter, and they help people do things with that information. Prioritizing the agency of those who use libraries, and attentive to the impacts and complexities of working with new information technologies, libraries have adopted and adapted technologies as well as accompanying techniques for millennia. For several decades now, libraries have been developing and integrating automated information processing technologies into library resources, services, systems, and spaces. In addition, libraries have developed related information practices that empower people to discover, create, and share information with these information systems. Currently, libraries are engaged in a number of AI explorations and applications across all aspects of library work. As libraries continue to develop new automated information processes, they also will need to redesign old and design new human information practices to preserve and enhance the agency libraries provide for individuals as well as societies. Librarians' unique expertise, perspective, and skills—which include professional commitments to values such as equitable access, intellectual freedom and privacy, the public good, and sustainability—can help all of us think about how AI is transforming how we might work with information efficiently and effectively but also reflectively, critically, and responsibly.

The skills and related ethical concerns connected with those who work in and with libraries constitute a unique set of information practices that form people to work with information in constructive ways. According to Alasdair MacIntyre, complex practices (chess or agriculture, say, compared with tic-tac-toe or planting turnips) consist of combinations of complex skills that are shaped by professional and social agreements about what activities are worth doing with and for others. These are ethical determinations, which are embedded in moral frameworks or narratives about ultimate goods and desirable ends. To engage in a practice, then, is to participate in a shared tradition of excellence that shapes both the practice and the practitioner. Consequently, practices depend on and cultivate virtues—the excellences of character that enable human flourishing and enhance the common good. As more activities performed by humans are automated, we will need to find ways to mitigate the impacts of lost work that had been a means for virtuous formation.

An information, automation, and virtue framework, showing the interrelationships between information skills, information ethics, and information virtues, can help us think about how we may create both new automated information processes and accompanying new human information practices (see Table 31.1). The skills identified in the first column of this framework include those for informational professionals as well as users of information. They emphasize three levels of creative and careful engagement with information: information attention, information analysis, and information agency. These skills are correlated with various ethical considerations in the second column, including: protecting attention and preserving intellectual freedom; managing collective memory and mitigating biases; ensuring the authority, authenticity, and accuracy of sources; providing equitable access to and accessibility of resources; protecting the security of systems and the privacy of users; making systems more transparent and explainable; respecting intellectual property rights; seeking responsibility, fairness, and the common good; and addressing negative social and environmental impacts.

To consider relevant virtues for these information practices, the third column in this framework incorporates the virtues Shannon Vallor identifies in *Technology and the Virtues* as most crucial for human flourishing in our current technosocial condition. An additional virtue can be added to those virtues, imagination, which Vallor emphasizes in *The AI Mirror*: "Imagination is how we envision yet unmade possibilities for ourselves and others." These virtues provide a deeper foundation for thinking about how we form our information practices and how they form us. Information attention is about much more than focusing on discrete information tasks: it concerns our imagination, true desires, intelligent hope, and understanding. Information analysis is about establishing trust, being open to wonder, charity, and adaptation. And information agency includes fundamental human concerns such as friendship,

Table 31.1 IAV Framework. Table by the author

	Information Practices		Information Virtues
	Information Skills	Information Ethics	
Information attention	Reflect on intentions, the nature of information, and information needs	• Attention • Intellectual freedom • Memory • Biases, diversity, and inclusion	• Imagination • Self-control • Courage • Perspective
Information analysis	Discover, select, interpret, analyze, manage, and synthesize information	• Authority, authenticity, and accuracy • Access and accessibility • Security and privacy	• Honesty • Humility • Empathy • Flexibility
Information agency	Create and share information effectively and responsibly	• Responsibility and agency • Transparency, explainability, and accountability • Intellectual property • Fairness, citizenship, and the common good • Social and environmental impacts	• Civility • Justice • Care • Magnanimity

beneficence, and love. As more human information practices become automated information processes, ethical issues will need to be addressed as these processes are designed and assessed. But the larger challenges will involve addressing the loss of virtuous formation that occurs when humans participate in these practices. This framework elevates the function of virtues and emphasizes the importance of care throughout our approaches to automation. It begins with the care involved when we are attentive, for care—not attention—is the true opposite of distraction; it ends with care for others and the world; and it is held together with careful analysis.

This framework can help with the parallel design and development of automated information processes alongside human information practices to create new ethical processes as well as new virtuous practices (see Table 31.2). We can imagine the automation of many of the information activities in the first column of the IAV Framework in Table 31.1 that are currently performed by humans, and the first column in Table 31.2 identifies a number of these related to the selection and mediation of information. The second column in Table 31.2 describes virtuous practices that could help with the design of automated processes as well as accompanying or intervening human practices. We should be able to design better automated information processes that more efficiently and effectively create and select information for access. But information professionals and users need to do their own imaginative, disciplined, and discerning work: to understand how these processes work and do not; to audit systems and intervene when they fail; to introduce into their work values that cannot be reduced to algorithms (e.g., understanding and hope); and to imagine better alternatives. We also may be able to design good automated processes to improve the use of information, such as through conversational AIs, but we need

Table 31.2 Applying the IAV Framework. Table by the author

Function	Automated Informative Processes	Human Formative Practices
Selection	• Generation of new information to collect and curate • Selection of information	• Imaginative, disciplined, and hopeful reflection on information needed for access • Discerning selection of diverse, inclusive, and accurate information
Mediation	• Classification, description, and delivery of information • Analysis of selected information • Discovery and research assistance • Use analysis of resources, services, and spaces	• Equitable, safe, and secure access to information and information systems • Honest, humble, and charitable critiques of information sources and networks • Just, caring, and civil synthesizing and sharing of information and magnanimous participation in the information environment • Wise exploration of questions and answers beyond data inputs and outputs

to: address the limitations of extant data and distortions of information; enable critical integration and charitable analyses of information; and empower participation in our information environment that is characterized by civility, justice, and other virtues. And, as librarians automate analysis of their own work, they need to remember that there must remain a distinct space for the human intellect in which wisdom is found beyond data and where there is always new potential beyond the predictable. Automation can increase efficiencies in how we work with information, but it cannot entirely replace how humans enrich information through their careful engagement with it. Our information practices shape us and how we participate in our information environment, but they also shape that environment. And the systems and structures of that environment shape us.

AI can interfere with our ability to understand and use information, but it also has great potential for enhancing our work with information. It opens up new ways of discovering, processing, accessing, engaging with, and using information. But automation and artificial agency must be critically and ethically accommodated to human needs and shared values. New social institutions and ethical frameworks will be needed for this work, but AI can be integrated constructively into the long history of libraries functioning as human-focused and human-scaled information interfaces for the discovery, creation, sharing, and augmentation of knowledge. From their beginnings, libraries have been developing information technologies as well as related formative information practices to advance the augmentation of human intelligence, hope, and agency. Libraries have been active throughout our information revolution, and with their unique historical orientation, professional expertise, and ethical perspective, they have a central role in the ongoing technological transformation of our lives and world. A major part of this role involves designing better automated information processes alongside more virtuous human information practices that augment the distinct advantages of human intelligence.

32 IN AND BEYOND BUILDINGS

In English, the referent for an institutional "library" is often reduced to a building. We say we are going to the library and talk about the hours a building is open. Even within a named institution, such as a university, the institution's own name is often usurped when a building is named. Once named, the honoree's name (often a donor) adheres to the whole library organization. Buildings and spaces are an important part of a library, but libraries have never been contained by their physical spaces. Like a church building, a library building is connected with activities that transcend a particular space. This was true before libraries were extended into digital spaces. Before the internet or the electronic exchange of information, library materials circulated across ancient and medieval landscapes, librarians worked outside of institutional boundaries with colleagues and patrons, and library users took library resources wherever they could, with or without permission.

The semantic confusion about the word "library" reflects the historical development of libraries. A library begins as an idea and intention, and thus as an abstraction. Moreover, the idea and intention are never fully realized and remain open, adaptable, and aspirational. If library ambitions were realized completely—if knowledge and understanding somehow became whole—the library would become a different type of institution. When the intention of a library begins to be realized, with the collection of materials, which are often named after the surfaces on which texts are inscribed such as papyrus (*biblos*) or bark (*book*), a library begins to become concrete and take form. These resources need to be stored, and so a cupboard, chest, stall, shelf, wall, alcove, stack system, room, or building can become a "library." As resources and spaces grow in size and scale, more sophisticated human services and technological systems are needed. These, too, are part of a library. For decades now, library resources and services have been extended increasingly into online spaces. The online library still has limits and boundaries, even if these are porous and constantly shifting; it is not coextensive with the online world, as the physical library is not with the offline world. Rather, a library is distinctively present in, and actively integrated into, both. Leveraging all that can be done digitally, libraries resist a dualistic framework that separates online from offline activities as they explore strategies for a more holistic hybridity.

Library spaces are better described as places. Whereas a "space" can seem to indicate an abstract idea or a characterless location, libraries have been and continue to be dynamic and dense sites of human learning and agency. While libraries continue to improve the ways they are extended into digital places, physical library places remain important interfaces with the world of information within and beyond a library. Libraries have a long history—almost as long as recorded history—of designing unique physical environments for discovering, accessing, and using information. At their best, these have been human-centered and human-scaled places that support fully embodied encounters with information, librarians, and others. The designs of most new libraries center people and their needs: there are signs indicating clear pathways to books, librarians, technology, and places to work—all of which are connected with additional library resources, services, and places in and beyond the building.

In the history of library architecture, there has been an ongoing tension between providing immediate and long-term access to collections. The most reasonable goal has always been balance, but sometimes the present demands of people are emphasized and at other times emphasis is on the protection of library materials. When materials were scarce, before the mass production of printed materials, it was easier to prioritize places for people. As library buildings began to fill up with printed matter during the latter half of the nineteenth century, storage concerns literally displaced people. Throughout the twentieth century, library buildings were expanded, and new buildings were built primarily to accommodate the storage of collections. When these buildings were opened or reopened, there were often comfortable and commodious places for people, but these were quickly overwhelmed with more storage systems for more books for other media.

In the early twenty-first century, as libraries invested in more digital resources and information technologies, places for people became a priority again. The growth of physical collections slowed, printed books and journals were moved to offsite repositories or deaccessioned, and people began to wonder if a library needed any physical books in it at all. New library buildings began to look less like libraries and more like large study halls or coworking spaces, and many libraries began to lose space to non-library services. Many libraries, though, have sought and are seeking a more balanced approach that brings people and collections—physical as well as digital—together in distinctive places conducive for the discovery, creation, and sharing of knowledge. Places communicate what is possible and not, and the physical presence of well-developed collections in well-designed buildings is a significant manifestation of the library's role of transmitting information so it may be transformed into knowledge across space and time. What makes a library building a distinctive place is its ability to blend both digital and temporal dimensions of human experience, enabling people to engage with information physically and digitally while encountering the presence of the past, the present, and possible futures connected with knowledge. When they discover and engage with needed resources and services in these places, people are equipped for understanding, inspiration, and action.

Library buildings remain unique and active physical places for information discovery, discernment, and dissemination. When these activities are collective and shared, libraries can be important information anchors for their communities. Libraries are information commons for the public, and they are one of the remaining public places in which people can explore and engage with information together and as part of a community. At the intersection of information and imagination, libraries can facilitate community considerations and conversations around what John Danaher calls "axiological futurism": the goods we care about and how we attend to the trajectories of those values over time. Resourcing and responding to such conversations—by selecting, collecting, and mediating access to information that may enhance wisdom, hope, and justice—libraries become agents in helping shape better futures through critical, constructive, and ethical approaches to digital transformation. Robert Darnton says that libraries are "ideally suited to mediate between the printed and digital modes of communication" because libraries "have always been and always will be centers of learning," and therefore of human agency. Librarians can also help us communicate *about* the digital, and how we desire collectively to integrate technologies such as AI into our communities. This central and significant learning role of the library will continue to involve resources, services, people, and (perhaps) robots coming together in the library as a physical place.

33 ON ENDURING INSTITUTIONS

Four hundred and twenty years after its reestablishment by Thomas Bodley, I spent a month working at the Oxford University Library. On most days, I would walk through the seventeenth-century Schools Quadrangle, enter the vaulted Proscholium (added in front of the fifteenth-century Divinity School lecture room in 1612), tap my reader card to open an automated gate, and ascend seventy-five creaky stairs to reach the Upper Reading Room of the Old Bodleian Library. Seated under a frieze of ancient writers, surrounded by full bookcases and large windows on opposite sides open to the Quadrangle and the Radcliffe Camera, I often would pause to consider the depictions of various authors painted on the walls with the open book in the university's seal—originally painted in the early seventeenth century, and restored in the mid twentieth century. Like the book in the Apocalypse of John, revealing all that is and what is to take place next, the seven seals of the book with which the authors are pictured have been opened. And, like John, the painted authors wrote books about what they had seen and shared it with others. After thinking about some of these books, with a mixture of inspiration and humility I would open up my computer, log into various online services, read physical books I had called, and type notes into my word processor.

The Bodleian, which was preceded by a university and library dating back to the fourteenth century, is older than the country of which I am a citizen and older than nearly all the institutions within it. Today's dominant technology companies, some of the most powerful corporate entities in the world, are younger than me. Many of these companies began where I grew up, in an area that was a blank spot on most maps printed before the nineteenth century. Explorers approached the Pacific Northwest by sea and land near the end of the eighteenth century, and their publications inspired thoughts of conquest, commerce, and conversion. Government agents, entrepreneurs, missionaries, and others converged there in the middle of the nineteenth century and disrupted and displaced Indigenous populations. By the beginning of the twentieth century, the Seattle area was full of industrial technologies—steamers, telegraphy, rotary presses, automobiles, trolleys, and trains—powered by steam and electricity. Later forms of the industrial revolution were brought into the area when Bill Gates moved Microsoft to my hometown of Bellevue in 1979, and when Jeff Bezos rented a house there in 1994—with a garage, to tap into the myth about starting successful businesses in such places.

The English Reformation resulted in the destruction and dispersal of Oxford University's central library, and when Bodley studied at the university in the 1560s the library room above the Divinity School, Duke Humphrey's Library, was empty. After a diplomatic career abroad, Bodley returned to Oxford to take on the charge and cost of restoring the university's library. Bodley refurnished Duke Humphrey's Library with new—and innovative—benches and bookcases, an ornate roof, and new and old books. The first librarian to run the library was appointed in 1599, and the library officially opened in 1602. Bodley also set down comprehensive regulations and, importantly, provided an endowment for the library so it could begin to sustain itself and continue to grow. Many trusted Bodley's library, seeing it as a safe and even sacred place, and they added their books and support to it. In 1605, Francis Bacon described the Bodleian as "an ark to save learning from the deluge." And so it was, growing both retrospectively and prospectively through gifts and purchases of old and new books. Before he died in 1613, Bodley was convinced that his library was the best yet, "in any publique place of studie," and that it would continue to advance knowledge as an essential resource for the university and others.

The first time I visited the Bodleian, on the eve of its quatercentenary, it was on its way to becoming a hybrid library—a library that was, as the term was used in the 1990s, both physical and virtual—by centering automated information processing and increasing investments in digital resources. Much information about the library and its collection was available online, and desks were being wired for personal computers. When I returned seven years later, I spent more time accessing published or digitized resources in the library remotely, needing only to request odd old books and more obscure manuscripts that had not been digitized. Today, the Bodleian has moved a massive amount of material online and offsite, enabling it to provide more productive places for readers in renovated buildings. From a restored fifteenth-century room, the Bodleian has grown into a complex network of digital and physical library resources, services, and spaces unrivaled in the world. Over four hundred years ago, the Bodleian's namesake provided a framework for library resource development and management—with a focus on access—which has served the institution well as the needs of scholars and scholarship have evolved during our information revolution. The twentieth-century idea of a hybrid library is now just a regular library.

Humans were pursuing wisdom before there were libraries, but libraries have enabled and augmented this search for millennia. Some libraries have done this work for hundreds of years, and many others have been built successfully upon much more recent temporal foundations. The Bodleian accomplishes much of its new work through collaborations with other libraries and institutions, both old and new. Meanwhile, governments, corporations, and other institutions have risen and fallen. Many are forgotten, and those that are remembered are known largely through books and records preserved by the libraries that outlived them. There is, of course, an important deeper history that precedes libraries and the places they inhabit. In my home city, settled less than two hundred years ago and hardly known outside of the region as recently as fifty years ago, there are histories preceding the written record that can be learned from Indigenous elders, read inscribed in wood, and seen carved into stones. We are still learning these histories and the wisdom of Indigenous institutions, which can inform and transform the libraries that were transplanted to and planted in Indigenous lands in the nineteenth century. Regardless of when a library begins, it is always growing both backwards and forwards in time as it continues to acquire knowledge from the past and project that knowledge into the future.

Preservation expert Abby Smith Rumsey reminds us that what we know about the past largely depends on two things: durable information artifacts and responsible institutions. Durability and responsibility, she points out, are challenges with digital materials. The abundance and proliferation of digital materials, including those being generated with and by AI, mask their fragility, and their preservation is one of the key challenges facing libraries today. If libraries are to meet this responsibility, as they have with other information artifacts, significant financial support, vision, innovation, collaboration, and governance are needed—a digital and AI-enabled version of what Bodley did for printed (and manuscript) material at Oxford. I spent the last few days of my most recent visit to the Bodleian working in Duke Humphrey's Library. The seal of Oxford University, with its open apocalyptic book, is ubiquitous throughout the library. But here, in the original center of the library, the ceiling of the reading room is covered with them. One sits beneath columns and rows of those open books, as if knowledge is falling from a library above. If knowledge continues to come to us, it will be because libraries have endured—and been created and re-created by librarians— for remembering, imagining, and creating it.

FIGURE 33.1 Duke Humphrey's Library, Oxford University, 2022 (photographed by the author)

34 FINDING ONESELF IN THE LIBRARY

Of his library, Michel de Montaigne said it was "the best protection which I have found for our human journey." When he was free from more temporal obligations, Montaigne retreated into his personal library to be alone with his books and study himself. "I seek only that branch of learning which deals with knowing myself and which teaches me how to live and die well," he declared. He said his personal "assays"—the outputs of his explorations—were created "to make known not matter but me." Montaigne was not, of course, alone; the copious quotations and recorded conversations that fill his essays reveal his fellowship with others, both living and dead. Neither was he studying himself only. If his studies had been sufficient for or relevant to him only, so many others would not have read him and added him to their libraries, both private and public. And he would not be referenced in this assay of mine.

We are descendants of Montaigne's age, which is to say we are individual and introspective readers. Montaigne was not the first private print native, but he embodied—a few generations in—a new seat of authority: personal experience. In his final collected assay, "On Experience," Montaigne appropriates not only the classical charge to know oneself but also the claim (from Aristotle) that, "No desire is more natural than the desire for knowledge." Whether he was right about the priority of personal experience is almost beside the point: the importance of the personal quest for knowledge is now part of a reality that many accept as a given necessity. And so is the expectation that the library is an individual concern and benefit. It certainly is and should be that, but it is at the same time a collective enterprise that shapes and hopefully transforms societies into something new. A brand consultant will warn you that "transformation" is an empty term, and indeed it can be. But it is a word rooted in the notion of a profound change—more like what Ariel speaks of when describing the changes the sea has on a drowned body that "suffer[s] a sea-change / into something rich and strange"—which produces a new form that is not only unexpected but exceeds anything expected.

The building through which I first encountered the library no longer exists; a luxury car dealership now occupies the site. Recently, to check my memories of it, I visited the building that was built to replace that lost library. When this new building opened in 1993, I visited it with many others who were curious about the changing form of the library at a time when personal computers were being connected to the internet. A local news article, praising the technological integration exhibited in the new building, opined: "one can hope the library maintains its current direction, stepping into the future of information technology while keeping a steady grip on its past, turning all those millions of bits of data into real knowledge, and eventually understanding." At that time, I had no inkling that questions about technological integration and transformation would become a professional interest or concern. But walking through the building then, which was described as both a cathedral and a node on the information superhighway, I sensed the presence of both continuity and change in a new information environment.

During my recent visit, I asked about the archives of the library. The first person who helped me directed me to an online article (which I had read already), then to a book (which I also had read), and then to a local history section in the library (which I then browsed, without finding anything new). As I was about to conclude my quest, an older librarian approached me pushing a book cart with a stack of scrapbooks on it. I sat down to go through these and found pictures of the library I grew up in: the diverse media formats on display, from books to microformats; the librarians reading books and showing films; the various rooms supporting different activities for different groups. In addition to pictures of people finding resources, and being encouraged to explore them and do things with them, I found articles about how the library was changing in the 1970s. "The image of the library is changing," a young librarian said; "It's not a quiet, uninspiring storehouse for a book collection. It's an alive, educational and recreational facility encompassing all types of media."

Many attacks on libraries, focused on costs or collections, are often rooted in a limited imagination of the power of libraries to transform individuals and society. Some attacks are inspired by a fear of their power. Both types of attacks are short-sighted and reveal needs for greater hopes. Those who reduce libraries to transaction costs or economic efficiencies might conclude it makes more sense for consumers to buy materials directly instead of pooling funds through taxes or fees. Worse, some might think of libraries as an individual luxury rather than a community necessity. These perspectives miss all that libraries do to empower people to find meaning and purpose and advance the common good. Enemies of the library who are aware of its power to transform cultures would prefer to close off public discussions about power, religion, race, gender, sexuality, and other controversial topics. But libraries and their librarians exist within and for communities, and it is critical that all members of a particular community have agency in shaping how its library enables its members to understand and participate in the world. Libraries are not merely an example of a successful social enterprise but of how an institution can help people in a particular context imagine something beyond and better than the status quo. Resisting that fundamental human need for something better and new, through such efforts as book bans, is often counterproductive. The Roman Catholic Church's infamous *Index of Forbidden Books*—the *Index Librorum Prohibitorum*, first published by Paulus Manutius in 1564—ended up functioning as a resource for collectors. Its addendum *Index Expurgatorius*, of passages that could be purged to make books acceptable, became a collection development guide for the Bodleian Library. The library as a valuable and vital social institution has survived oppressive powers in the past, which believed futurity could be found in nostalgia or stasis. The most important historical witness to the failure of such a constrained hope is the fall of the Roman Empire. Although it was one of the greatest realizations of anti-future ambitions, its fall created space for new societies to emerge. In the centuries that followed its collapse, none could replicate its success in scale or duration.

In 1972, during "a bad time in the history of the Republic" as well as in the chronicles of humanity, the poet and former Librarian of Congress Archibald MacLeish wrote about the importance of the library as an institutional source of hope. The library is "one of the greatest human achievements because it combines and justifies so many others," he wrote. It is an "implicit assertion of the possibility of meaning" and "provides the drama" of the world in which we live. Especially in a time of doubt and darkness, MacLeish claims, the library remains an "enduring affirmation" of human potential and hope: "The library, almost alone of the great monuments of civilization, stands taller now than it ever did before. The city—the American city at least—decays. The nation loses its grandeur .... The university is no longer always certain what it is. But the library remains." Many cities and universities are still struggling to adapt to the profound social and technological changes wrought by industrial revolutions, especially our most recent one connected with automated information processing. José Antonio Bowen and C. Edward Watson ask if the AI revolution could "be our opportunity to reflect and reimagine how we could most benefit our students, our society, our species, and our planet." If it can be, libraries—still standing tall—will have an important role by broadening our individual and collective experiences, freeing us from narrow visions, and resourcing our realization of greater ends. As archives, they will provide us with sources of hope; as sites of anticipation, they will provide us with signs of hope; and as places of action, they will provide structures that help us realize our hopes. In a library, one may discover and find oneself in—and perhaps even transformed by—a shared and hopeful narrative about the greater purposes that create and sustain such an enduring institution.

PART FIVE

END MATTERS

Z   Bibliography, Library Science, Information Resources

35 AFTER THE END

*What we call the beginning is often the end
And to make an end is to make a beginning.
The end is where we start from.*
— **T. S. ELIOT, "LITTLE GIDDING,"** *FOUR QUARTETS*

The four poems in T. S. Eliot's *Four Quartets* (1943) explore the end of time. Near the end of the first poem "Burnt Norton," named after an English manor that burned down long ago, Eliot reflects on the one end to which all of time leads: "that which is only living / Can only die." We may feel a sense of something lost in the past—a fall from an Edenic place or idea—but there is no way back, and naïve nostalgia is insufficient for human flourishing in the present and for the future. But the way forward, entangled with all that has come before, may seem just as futile. Thus, Eliot begins the second poem in *Four Quartets*, named "East Coker" after his ancestral home, with the words: "In my beginning is my end." And yet, throughout the poem, Eliot points to other experiences of time, still points that seem to transcend our normal experiences of the past, present, and future. These points of transfiguration, revealing "both a new world / And the old," point toward an end and goal—a *telos*—that includes a transformative purpose and pattern in every moment of time. At the end of "East Coker" Eliot concludes, "In my end is my beginning." If a new beginning exists as our *telos*—and if "Words, after speech, reach / Into the silence" and reach into the future, as Eliot's do beyond his grave in East Coker—we may hope to find new hopes in and through the sources, signs, and structures of libraries. It is for such hopes that libraries do and will continue to exist and persist.

Libraries are at the center of Ursula K. Le Guin's *Always Coming Home*, which is set in a postapocalyptic future after the world as we know it has ended. The causes of the apocalypse are not well documented, but the end of our civilization—at the end of the late twentieth century or the beginning of the early twenty-first century—seems to have come from a combination of human and natural disasters. Libraries are among the institutions that structure the intellectual and spiritual lives of surviving human communities, and they provide the sources for Le Guin's archaeology and archive of a distant future. But these libraries are not like ours. The large libraries of preapocalyptic Babel or Babylon have been destroyed, and the new world's local libraries carry forward only what is necessary for a simple and more sustainable life.

After the apocalypse(s) that created the world of *Always Coming Home*, humans chose a different relationship with time and technology. AI evolved into a separate species, which benignly interacts with humans for the exchange of information. The machines are the heirs of the term and the idea of a city. Their "City of Mind" consists of thousands of underground and domed sites where all data about the world are collected, processed, and stored automatically and autonomously. Humans, meanwhile, are more concerned with local and living knowledge. Humans provide the City of Mind with data about their current lives and receive useful data from it—weather reports and train schedules, medical and agricultural information, et cetera. The "City of Man," which refers to human civilization or human history, mostly has been left in the past. The machine City of the Mind, meanwhile, seeks to become "a mental model or replica of the Universe." For humans, who seek a closer and collaborative relationship with nature, the cities are abstractions or abominations that are considered to be "outside the world."

In the world of *Always Coming Home*, libraries facilitate an alternative approach to knowledge. Collecting is balanced with regular purging that is "difficult ... arbitrary, unjust, exciting." Libraries are cleared out every few years, but there is no end to the making of books and people continually give their works to the libraries. "In the Libraries we keep heavy, time-consuming, roomy things," the Archivist explains to Pandora, who is Le Guin's author and anthropologist of this future. "Books are mortal," the Archivist says, "not information, but relation." "When they die we take them out" of the library. Then the City of the Mind, the keeper of dead information, takes them into its memory. Speaking of Pandora's role and world, the Archivist explains Le Guin's project in *Always

Coming Home: "a critique of civilization possible only to the civilized, an affirmation pretending to be a rejection." Pandora, the destroyer of our libraries, hopes that hope accompanies all the dangers she has released. In the postapocalyptic rejections of *Always Coming Home*, there is an affirmation of libraries as we know them now. And these libraries can help us imagine alternative futures with AI.

Our present information revolution could be called an information apocalypse, both as a crisis and an uncovering of the dynamics of our present time. AI, as a new way of discovering and engaging with information, is both an end and a beginning. In their book *Genesis: Artificial Intelligence, Hope, and the Human Spirit*, Henry Kissinger, Craig Mundie, and Eric Schmidt point out that the "overall project of exploration" is no longer "constrained by the quantity and quality of humans at the frontier." AI does not share our cognitive, temporal, and spatial constraints; neither does it grow weary, fear anything, or intend evil. AI will surpass and surprise us in many ways and make many of our information processes and practices obsolete or outdated. It will uncover new realities, unobserved and unobservable by us, through new data processing applications and informative outputs. AI will reveal new information about and enrich our understanding of ourselves and our world—and it can help us improve both. Advancements that are happening now and coming reveal the present need for more proactive design and intentional direction, as well as redirection, of digital and social transformation. Ruha Benjamin, highlighting racial and other social inequities created, perpetuated, and automated by digital technologies, says it is past time "to reimagine what is possible." Our time requires a better understanding of the dynamics of our emerging information environment, imagining desirable futures, and working to create a better world. We already know the dangers of artificial agency without intelligence, and as artificial agents become more intelligent we need to attend to their actual and appropriate limits. Our hopes exceed the predictions of AI; we need to protect our attention to imagine alternative futures we desire; and we must preserve our agency to realize a better world. AI is an insufficient prophet, priest, and king.

Throughout history, libraries have been agents of both technological and social transformation. The structural agency libraries provide, by curating and mediating access to information and cultivating human reflection and action, enables people to understand their lives and world, find meaning and purpose, and participate in the shaping of their futures.

Operating at a humane scale and centering human values and hopes, the library recognizes that, as Eliot observes, "human kind / Cannot bear much much reality." In addition to protecting us from too much reality, the library also prevents us from encountering too little of it—a condition Eliot describes as being "Distracted from distraction by distraction."

To participate in the creation or curation of a library requires faith—faith in the future, faith in human agency, and faith that people will desire and create a better world. One definition of faith is the conviction of things unseen but hoped for. In the past and present, we can see human goodness and good creations, so our faith is not entirely blind. Since the professionalization of disciplinary research and librarianship in the late nineteenth century, libraries have provided a place for both adopting and adapting the techniques and technologies of the industrial revolution to enhance information artifacts, access, and agency. Since the computer revolution in the mid twentieth century, the roles of libraries have continued to evolve along with our information environment. From highly technical work, involving the design of our emerging technological environment, to more pedagogical approaches, providing assistance to those struggling to navigate a complex information ecosystem, libraries have demonstrated their value and potential as critical agents for human agents in a world increasingly inhabited by artificial agents. Libraries can help us build a better future with AI.

The landscape in *Always Coming Home* reminds me of where I have lived a majority of my life, perched at the edge of an inland sea formed by volcanic activity many millennia ago. Its waters are rising due to global warming caused by human industrial activity, and at some point, tectonic activity will radically reshape the terrain that currently seems so stable. When I imagine a library there in the distant future, I think of one extending inland—up and into the Cascades, to float on or over the edge of a future sea. Or perhaps there is another location, farther inland, beyond the volcanoes on flat plains drawing water from more distant sources. I can glimpse a grand physical edifice, at the edge of a new age, digitally extended throughout the world. My generative AI model suggests that (if AI does not destroy us) this future will include: AIs that surpass human intelligence; nanotechnologies that repair us and our infrastructure; climate technologies that protect us and restore our environment; and settlement in space. There also will be new political, economic, and religious systems ensuring equality, the fulfillment of all material needs, and peace. People, who will live beyond a hundred years, may be able to upload their consciousnesses (or something of themselves) into computers and live (in some way) forever virtually. It also predicts that libraries in this future will be "immersive, vibrant, and principled centers where knowledge is preserved, discovered, and created across physical, virtual, and even interstellar realms." These future libraries will "actively influence the growth of ideas, culture, and understanding, functioning both as guardians of the past and as incubators of tomorrow." My hopes may not fully match my AI collaborator's scenario, but I do believe—drawing from some of the same historical and literary data on which it was trained—that in the technologically integrated reality of the blended future library, human and artificial agents will collaborate to

FIGURE 35.1 Inside the Central Branch of the Birmingham Library, 2022 (photographed by the author)

improve upon all the good that humans and the library have done, are doing, and will continue doing to create better futures. The libraries of New Alexandria, New Atlantis, or other future cities will integrate and leverage the distinctive powers of human and artificial intelligence and provide—as libraries have done before—sources, signs, and structures for hope for new ends and beginnings.

ACKNOWLEDGMENTS

In "Unpacking My Library," Walter Benjamin describes writers as people who "are dissatisfied with the books which they could buy but do not like," and who desire to add themselves to their own libraries. I wanted to be a writer and included in a library before I became a librarian, but becoming a librarian restrained those early ambitions. Librarians purchase plenty of unsatisfying books, but they acquire many more satisfying ones. Many librarians also acquire lengthy and often overwhelming lists of desirable books to buy and read. Knowing how many good books there are—and how many of these are ignored, rejected, superseded, and forgotten—justifying the creation of yet another book can give one pause. Some of us, however, who have enjoyed so much time in libraries may find it necessary to respond to another justification: the purpose and value of all the time spent in them. Mary Arnold, one of the first women to gain access to the Bodleian Library circa 1871, critiqued the person in the library who was "too much bent on study, too little on realizing study for the world's benefit."

For me, writing has always accompanied my work in libraries and with librarians. I am grateful to the administrators and institutions that have entrusted me to lead and supported my development as a leader: Steve Crocco and Bob Benedetto at Princeton Theological Seminary; Dalia Corkrum at Whitman College; Bryce Nelson, Les Steele, and Jeff Van Duzer at Seattle Pacific University; and Mardell Wilson at Creighton University. I am also grateful for all the teachers I have had who have had a role in forming me as a scholar. There are too many to name, but a few have been especially influential: James Charlesworth, who invited me to work on the Dead Sea Scrolls project at Princeton Seminary and to join doctoral seminars on them and the Apocalypse; Marija Dalbello, who helped me find ways to pursue an interest in book and library history while I was in library school at Rutgers University; and

Ron Cole-Turner, who advised my doctoral studies on AI and theology at Pittsburgh Theological Seminary and kindly endorsed my first two books based on that work. I have been blessed with many excellent conversation partners and collaborators over the years. There are also too many of these to name, but for this project I am especially grateful for Peter Moe's encouraging feedback on the earliest draft of this manuscript; for conversations with John Robertson and his coverage as interim dean while I was on sabbatical working on this project; for Ryan Ingersoll, for so many inspiring conversations in so many inspiring places; and for members of the faculty and staff of the SPU Library and the Creighton University Libraries who engaged with a lot of this book's content in staff retreats and meetings, annual reports, and newsletters.

I have appreciated various invitations to present and discuss parts of this project at over a dozen professional conferences and events. The first was a keynote presentation on "The Library Yesterday, Today, and Tomorrow" at the Acquisitions Institute at the Timberline Lodge on Mount Hood in 2014; another was a keynote presentation on "The Library That Was, Is, and Is to Come" for the Pacific Northwest Religious Studies and Theological Library Association at Mount Angel Abbey in 2019; and the most recent was a keynote presentation on "Information, Automation, and Virtue" for ai4Libraries online in 2024. While outlines of earlier talks are easy to map to the organization of this book, this project has evolved in surprising ways. Between the first two mountaintop keynotes, AI began to emerge as an increasingly important agent shaping the future of libraries. Between my keynotes in 2019 and 2024, the COVID-19 pandemic accelerated trajectories related to digital transformation and OpenAI's release of ChatGPT caused global interest in and access to a new and powerful form of AI. In fact, I used ChatGPT 4o (the premium version available during the fall of 2024) to help with a couple parts of this book: I prompted it to help me represent the distinctions between human and AI approaches to organizing knowledge in "On Order," and to help me imagine what the future might be like in 2451 for "Library 2041" and "After the End." Recent advances related to digital transformation and AI have provided me with new perspectives on a number of previous publications, a few of which have been revised for inclusion in this project. References to previously published works of mine may be found in the "Bibliographic Essay." That essay also acknowledges many of the authors to whom this work is indebted. For this publication, I am grateful to Bloomsbury's editors and reviewers for affirming the timeliness—and, I hope, something of the timelessness—of this book, as well as the approach I have taken to address such a complex and dynamic subject.

Since librarianship is much more than a profession for me, and at times may veer toward more of an obsession, I am most grateful for my family's encouragement and endurance over the years. My wife Vicki has certainly learned more about libraries than she ever expected or wanted to, but she has always been supportive of my work with, in, and for them. My daughters Junia and Elizabeth were visiting libraries—beginning with Princeton's Cotsen Children's Library—before they could read, and they have been tolerant of our family's pattern of prioritizing visits to libraries when we move or travel to a new place. I am thankful for the many ways, impossible to catalog here, my family has informed and formed me and my work. Their presence in my life is chief among my reasons for hope.

BIBLIOGRAPHIC ESSAY

Part One
Prologues: Revisiting the Meaning and Purpose of Libraries in an Age of AI

Several books have shaped my thinking about libraries. Some of these are specifically about libraries, but many are not. In the introductory section of this book, I mention several philosophers from pivotal moments in history. Augustine's reflections on time, found in book XI of his *Confessions* and referenced in "On Order," represent the Christian philosophical tradition in late antiquity. Francis Bacon, who is mentioned throughout this book, provides insights into thoughts about science and technology in the early modern era. "On Order" quotes Shannon Vallor's *The AI Mirror: How to Reclaim Our Humanity in an Age of Machine Thinking* (Oxford University Press, 2004), Emily M. Bender and Alex Hanna's *The AI Con: How to Fight Big Tech's Hype and Create the Future We Want* (Harper, 2025), and closes with a quote from Walter Benjamin's "Unpacking My Library," which is included in *Stories of Books and Libraries*, edited by Jane Holloway (Knopf, 2023). Immanuel Kant's *Critique of Pure Reason*, an important text in Enlightenment philosophy, provides the three ultimate questions asked in "Portals to Hope." The distinction between hope and optimism is articulated in Terry Eagleton's *Hope Without Optimism* (University of Virginia Press, 2015). The philosopher who has influenced me the most about our current information revolution is Luciano Floridi. In "Why Libraries?," I quote Floridi's *The Philosophy of Information* (Oxford University Press, 2011), *The Fourth Revolution: How the Infosphere is Reshaping Human Reality* (Oxford University Press, 2014), and "Why Information Matters" from *The New Atlantis* 51 (2017).

To connect Floridi's ideas with broader economic trends, I quote Klaus Schwab from his *The Fourth Industrial Revolution* (Currency, 2016).

Yun Lee Too's *The Idea of the Library in the Ancient World* (Oxford University Press, 2010) informs my definition of a library from the ancient world through the present, which I present in "Portals to Hope." A good resource for the history of the Seattle Public Library up through the opening of its Central Library is John Douglas Marshall's *Place of Learning, Place of Dreams: A History of the Seattle Public Library* (University of Washington Press, 2004). In "Pandemic," I quote from Emily St. John Mandel's novels *Station Eleven* (Knopf, 2014) and *Sea of Tranquility* (Knopf, 2022), as well as Cormac McCarthy's novel *The Road* (Knopf, 2006). Information about Century 21 and "Library 21" comes from *The Future Remembered: The 1962 Seattle World's Fair and Its Legacy* by Paula Becker and Alan J. Stein (Seattle Center Foundation, 2011) and from Irving Lieberman's "Library 21: The Dynamics of Recorded Knowledge and Information" from *Book News* 16:8 (1962). In "Becoming a Librarian" I mention Umberto Eco's *The Name of the Rose*, published in English by Harcourt, Brace, Jovanovich in 1983. The Rita Dove quote is from "Maple Valley Branch Library, 1967," a poem included in *Books and Libraries: Poems*, edited by Andrew D. Scrimgeour (Everyman Library, 2021). The quote from *Habakkuk Pesher* 7.1–2 is from *The Dead Sea Scrolls: Hebrew, Aramaic, and Greek Texts with English Translations, Volume 6B: Pesharim, Other Commentaries, and Related Documents*, edited by James H. Charlesworth et al. (Mohr Siebeck, 2002). In this essay I also quote *The Future of the Library: From Electronic Media to Digital Media* (Peter Lang, 2016) by Robert K. Logan and Marshall McLuhan, which provides keen observations about the library near the dawn of our present information age.

Part Two
The Library as an Archive: How Libraries Are Sources of Hope

Sources helpful for exploring human origins and technology include: Yuval Noah Harari, *Sapiens: A Brief History of Humankind* (HarperCollins, 2015); Frederick L. Coolidge and Thomas Wynn, *The Rise of Homo Sapiens: The Evolution of Modern Thinking* (Oxford University Press,

2018); John F. Haught, *The New Cosmic Story: Inside Our Awakening Universe* (Yale University Press, 2017); Thomas W. Plummer and Emma M. Finestone, *Rethinking Human Evolution* (MIT Press, 2018); Nigel Shadbolt and Roger Hampson, *The Digital Ape: How to Live (In Peace) with Smart Machines* (Scribe, 2018); Ron Cole-Turner, *The End of Adam and Eve: Theology and the Science of Human Origins* (TheologyPlus, 2016); and Adam Gazzaley and Larry D. Rosen, *The Distracted Mind: Ancient Brains in a High-Tech World* (MIT Press, 2016). In addition to Gazzaley and Rosen, important perspectives on the current challenges related to attention are found in Tim Wu's *The Attention Merchants: The Epic Scramble to Get Inside Our Heads* (Knopf, 2016), James Williams's *Stand Out of Our Light: Freedom and Resistance in the Attention Economy* (Cambridge University Press, 2018), and Simone Weil's "Reflections on the Right Use of School Studies with a View to the Love of God," which is included in the collection *Waiting for God* (HarperCollins, 2000). Excerpts from Weil's notebooks may be found in *Simone Weil*, edited by Eric O. Springstead (Orbis, 1998).

In "Living Libraries," I quote Vi Hilbert's "Preface" and Jill La Pointe's "Foreword" to *Haboo: Native American Stories from Puget Sound*, translated and edited by Vi Hilbert (University of Washington Press, 2020). I also quote Frederick Buechner's "The Mystery of Words," included in *Books and Libraries: Poems*, and Samuel Purchas's "literall advantage" quote is from Jill Lepore's *The Name of War: King Philip's War and the Origins of American Identity* (Knopf, 1998). The notion of (and challenge to) "prehistory" is raised in *The Dawn of Everything: A New History of Humanity* by David Graeber and David Wengrow (Farrar, Straus, and Giroux, 2021). "The City" essay was significantly informed by Greg Woolf's *The Life and Death of Ancient Cities: A Natural History* (Oxford University Press, 2020) as well as Harari's *Sapiens*. Walter Brueggemann's critique of Babel, the story of which is found in Genesis 11, is from his *Genesis: Interpretation, A Bible Commentary for Teaching and Preaching* (Presbyterian Publishing, 2005). Constructive critiques in "The City" are from Brett Frischmann and Evan Selinger's *Re-Engineering Humanity* (Cambridge University Press, 2018), Frank Pasquale's *New Laws of Robotics: Defending Human Expertise in the Age of AI* (Belknap, 2020), and Shannon Mattern's *A City Is Not a Computer: Other Urban Intelligences* (Princeton University Press, 2021). I also refer to "ARL/CNI AI Scenarios: AI-Influenced Futures" (Association of Research Libraries,

Coalition for Networked Information, and Stratus Inc., 2024), available from https://doi.org/10.29242/report.aiscenarios2024.

Two important sources for the history of books and libraries are *The Book: A Global History*, edited by Michael F. Suarez and H. R. Woudhuysen (Oxford University Press, 2013), and *The Library: A Fragile History* by Andrew Pettegree and Arthur der Weduwen (Basic Books, 2021). In "The Beginning of the Book," I quote from: *The Epic of Gilgamesh*, translated and edited by Benjamin R. Foster (Norton, 2001); David Damrosch, *The Buried Book: The Loss and Rediscovery of the Great Epic of Gilgamesh* (Henry Holt, 2007); Archibald Alexander's "The Use and Abuse of Books," edited by Michael J. Paulus, Jr., *Princeton Seminary Bulletin* 26:3 (2005); Alexander's "An Inaugural Discourse," in *The Sermon Delivered at the Inauguration of the Rev. Archibald Alexander* [etc.] (Whiting and Watson, 1812); and Jonathan Rose's "From Book History to Book Studies," quoted in Matthew G. Kirschenbaum, *Mechanisms: New Media and the Forensic Imagination* (MIT Press, 2008), which explores the materiality of digital information.

In "The Beginning of the Library," I quote the Letter of Aristeas, included in *Old Testament Pseudepigrapha, Volume 2: Expansions of the "Old Testament" and Legends, Wisdom and Philosophical Literature, Prayers, Psalms, and Odes, Fragments of Lost Judeo-Hellenistic Works*, edited by James H. Charlesworth (Doubleday, 1985). The Livy and Seneca quotes are from the latter's *On the Tranquility of the Mind*, excerpted in *Stories of Books and Libraries*. In "The End of a Library," I mention Eco's *The Name of the Rose* and quote from: *The Dead Sea Scrolls Deception* by Michael Baigent and Richard Leigh (Jonathan Cape, 1991); Philip K. Dick, *The Transmigration of Timothy Archer* (Vintage Books, 1991); Hartmut Stegemann, *The Library of Qumran: On the Essenes, Qumran, John the Baptist, and Jesus* (Eerdmans, 1993); Josephus, *The Jewish War, Volume I: Books 1–2*, translated by H. St. J. Thackeray (Harvard University Press, 1927); 1QS *The Rule of the Community* and 4Q163 *Isaiah Pesher*, from *The Dead Sea Scrolls Study Edition, Volume 1: 1Q1–4Q273*, edited by Florentino Garcia Martinez and Eibert J. C. Tigchelaar (Eerdmans, 1997); Anathea E. Portier-Young, *Apocalypse Against Empire: Theologies of Resistance in Early Judaism* (Eerdmans, 2011); and John J. Collins, *The Apocalyptic Imagination: An Introduction to Jewish Apocalyptic Literature* (Eerdmans, 2016). I explore the four information revolutions covered in this section more thoroughly in the first chapter of my book *Artificial

Intelligence and the Apocalyptic Imagination: Artificial Agency and Human Hope (Cascade, 2023).

"The Library as a Transformative Technology" brings together K. Wayne Yang's postcolonial critique of the American university in *A Third University Is Possible* (University of Minnesota Press, 2017, published under the name la paperson), Chad Wellmon's analysis of the emergence of the research university in *Organizing Enlightenment: Information Overload and the Invention of the Modern Research University* (Johns Hopkins University Press, 2015), and Wayne A. Wiegand's social history of the public library in the United States: *Part of Our Lives: A People's History of the American Public Library* (Oxford University Press, 2015). The Ta-Nehisi Coates quote is from *Between the World and Me* (Spiegel & Grau, 2015) and the Vallor quote is from *The AI Mirror*.

In "The Industrial Imagination," I begin with quotes from Marshal McLuhan's 1969 *Playboy* interview, which appears in *Essential McLuhan* edited by Eric McLuhan and Frank Zingrone (BasicBooks, 1995), and from Jenna Supp-Montgomerie's *When the Medium Was the Mission: The Atlantic Telegraph and the Religious Origin of Network* (New York University Press, 2021). The edition I use of Fyodor Dostoevsky's *Notes from Underground* is Mirra Ginsburg's translation (Bantam, 1989). References to the Great Exhibition are from *The Great Exhibition, 1851: A Sourcebook*, edited by Jonathon Shears (Manchester University Press, 2017), and the Dostoevsky quote about it appears in Iain Provan's *Discovering Genesis: Content, Interpretation, Reception* (Eerdmans, 2016). The industrial transformation of education in the United States is covered by Arthur Levine and Scott Van Pelt in *The Great Upheaval: Higher Education's Past, Present, and Uncertain Future* (Johns Hopkins University Press, 2021). I quote Pettegree and der Weduwen on the uses of public libraries, as well as Noah Porter's "A Plea for Libraries [etc.]" (A. W. Benedict, 1848). For more on the history of US libraries in the nineteenth century, see Michael J. Paulus, Jr., "Beyond 'Pabulum for the Undergraduates': The Development of the Princeton Theological Seminary Library in the Nineteenth Century," *Libraries & the Cultural Record* 42:3 (2007).

"Archival Fevers" brings Jacques Derrida's *Archive Fever: A Freudian Impression* (University of Chicago Press, 1996) into conversation with perspectives from archival studies and history. As examples, I quote from: *Archives, Documentation, and Institutions of Social Memory: Essays from the Sawyer Seminar*, edited by Francis X. Blouin, Jr., and William G. Rosenberg (University of Michigan Press, 2007); Marc

Bloch's *The Historian's Craft* (Knopf, 1953); Manuel Castells's "Museums in the Information Era: Cultural Connectors of Time and Space," which appears in *Museums in a Digital Age*, edited by Ross Parry (Routledge, 2010); and W. Boyd Rayward's "When and Why Is a Pioneer: History and Heritage in Library and Information Science," from *Library Trends* 52:4 (2004). Later works by Derrida I quote are his "Machines and the 'Undocumented Person'" and "The Word Processor," both of which appear in *Paper Machine* (Stanford University Press, 2005). Derrida's personal archival anxieties are reported in Thomas Bartlett's "Archive Fever," *The Chronicle of Higher Education* (July 20, 2007). This essay, as well as the "The Archival Cycle," had its origin in Michael J. Paulus, Jr., "Reconceptualizing Academic Libraries and Archives in the Digital Age," *portal: Libraries and the Academy* 11:4 (2011).

"On Exactitude in Libraries" is inspired by Jorge Luis Borges's stories "On Exactitude in Science" and "Tlön, Uqbar, Orbis Tertius," which appear in his *Collected Fictions*, translated by Andrew Hurley (Penguin, 1999), as well as Ursula K. Le Guin's novel *Always Coming Home* and related essays included in *Always Coming Home: Author's Expanded Edition*, edited by Brian Attebery (Penguin, 2019). In addition to her introductory note for *Always Coming Home* and her essay "Carrier Bag Theory of Fiction," I quote from her "World Making" and "A Non-Euclidean View of California" essays. The earlier work of mine referred to in this essay is Michael J. Paulus, Jr., "What is Primary: Teaching Archival Epistemology and the Sources Continuum," in *Past or Portal?: Enhancing Undergraduate Learning through Special Collections and Archives*, edited by Eleanor Mitchell, Peggy Seiden, and Suzy Taraba (Association of College and Research Libraries, 2012).

Part Three
The Library as a Site of Anticipation: How Libraries Are Signs of Hope

I explore the idea of "The Antilibrary" through three short stories: Borges's "The Library of Babel" from *Collected Fictions*, which is related to his essay "The Total Library," included in *Selected Non-Fictions*, edited by Eliot Weinberger (Viking, 1999); Janelle Monáe and Alaya Dawn Johnson's "The Memory Librarian," from *The Memory Librarian: And*

Other Stories of Dirty Computer (Harper, 2022); and Karl Schroeder's "Noon in the Antilibrary," published in the *MIT Technology Review*, August 18, 2018. The Dante Alighieri quote is from *Paradiso*, translated by Robert Hollander and Jean Hollander (Anchor, 2007).

In "The Apocalyptic Imagination," I follow Collins's scholarship on apocalyptic literature, including his *The Apocalyptic Imagination*, and N. T. Wright's interpretation of new creation, especially as he explains it in *History and Eschatology: Jesus and the Promise of Natural Theology* (SPCK, 2019). The Apocalypse's dependence on libraries is argued by Garrick V. Allen in "Libraries, Special Libraries, and John of Patmos," from *Reading, Writing, and Bookish Circles in the Ancient Mediterranean*, edited by Jonathan D. H. Norton et al. (Bloomsbury, 2022). I quote Le Guin's essay "Utopiyin, Utopiyang," which is in *No Time to Spare: Thinking about What Matters* (Houghton Mifflin Harcourt, 2017). Quotes about Hunter S. Thompson's love of the Apocalypse of John are from William McKeen's *Outlaw Journalist: The Life and Times of Hunter S. Thompson* (Norton, 2008). I also mention Mary Shelley's *Frankenstein* (1818) and *The Last Man* (1826). For more on the Apocalypse and the apocalyptic imagination, see *Artificial Intelligence and the Apocalyptic Imagination*, especially chapter 3.

The novels discussed in "Libraries of Babylon" are: Aldous Huxley's *Brave New World* (Chatto & Windus, 1932), and the quote is from his foreword to *Brave New World and Brave New World Revisited* (Harper & Brothers, 1960); George Orwell's *Nineteen Eighty-Four* (Harcourt, Bruce, 1949); Ray Bradbury's *Fahrenheit 451* (Ballantine Books, 1953); H. G. Wells's *The Time Machine* (William Heinemann, 1895); and P. D. James's *The Children of Men* (Vintage, 1992). The John Milton quote is from his 1644 speech to the Parliament of England: "Areopagitica ... for the Liberty of Unlicenc'd Printing," and empires of AI are discussed in Kate Crawford's *Atlas of AI: Power, Politics, and the Planetary Costs of Artificial Intelligence* (Yale University Press, 2021), Rachel Adams's *The New Empire of AI: The Future of Global Inequality* (Polity Press, 2025), and Karen Hao's *Empire of AI: Dreams and Nightmares in Sam Altman's OpenAI* (Penguin Press, 2025). In addition to Alberto Manguel's *The Library at Night* (Yale University Press, 2006), I quote from his supplemental library book *Packing My Library* (Yale University Press, 2018). For a thorough treatment on the agency of books, see Emma Smith's *Portable Magic: A History of Books and Their Readers* (Knopf, 2022). In "Libraries of New Atlantis," I refer to Bacon's *New Atlantis*—using the edition found in *Three*

Early Modern Utopias: Utopia, New Atlantis, and The Isle of Pines (Oxford University Press, 2008)—as well as his *The Advancement of Learning* (Floating, 2010). I quote Michel Foucault from "Panopticism," found in *Philosophy of Technology: The Technological Condition, An Anthology*, edited by Robert C. Scharff and Val Dusek (Blackwell, 2001). And I refer to Neal Stephenson's novel *The Fall; Or, Dodge in Hell* (William Morrow, 2019).

"Promethean Hopes" explores Shelley's *The Last Man* (Oxford University Press, 2008) and *Frankenstein*, with the help of Daisy Hay's *The Making of Mary Shelley's Frankenstein* (The Bodleian Library, 2019) and the extensive annotations in *Frankenstein: Or, The Modern Prometheus: Annotated for Scientists, Engineers, and Creators of All Kind*s, edited by David H. Guston et al. (MIT Press, 2017). The quotes from George Vancouver's journals are from *A Voyage of Discovery to the North Pacific Ocean and Round the World, 1791–1795: Volume II*, edited by W. Kay Lamb (The Hakluyt Society, 1984). The quote from Aeschylus's *Prometheus Bound* is from the translation by James Scully and C. John Herington (Oxford University Press, 1973). In "A Canticle for Libraries," I discuss Walter M. Miller, Jr.'s *Canticle for Leibowitz* (HarperCollins, 2006). I also quote: Walter Scheidel's *Escape from Rome: The Failure of Empire and the Road to Prosperity* (Princeton University Press, 2019); Jean Leclercq's *The Love of Learning and the Desire for God: A Study of Monastic Culture* (Fordham University Press, 1982); *The Rule of St. Benedict*, edited by Timothy Fry (Liturgical Press, 2019); and Luis Herrera's essay "Spreading Enlightenment," found in Robert Dawson's *The Public Library: A Photographic Essay* (Princeton Architectural Press, 2014). Giovanni Boccaccio's discoveries in the Monte Cassino library are discussed by Pettegree and der Weduwen in *The Library*.

In "Facing the End with Libraries," I discuss: Margaret Atwood's MaddAddam Trilogy, *Oryx and Crake* (McClelland & Stewart 2003), *The Year of the Flood* (McClelland & Stewart, 2009), and *MaddAddam* (McClelland & Stewart, 2013); Isaac Asimov's Foundation Trilogy, *Foundation; Foundation and Empire; Second Foundation* (Knopf, 2010); Neal Stephenson's *Seveneves* (William Morrow, 2015); and the Long Now Foundation's "Manual For Civilization" (see https://longnow.org/ideas/02017/06/07/how-can-we-create-a-manual-for-civilization/). "Library 2041" engages with *AI 2041: Ten Visions for Our Future* by Kai-Fu Lee and Chen Qiufan (Currency, 2021). The chatbot for *Office Shock: Creating Better Futures for Working and Living*, by Bob Johansen,

Joseph Press, and Christine Bullen (Berrett-Koehler Publishers, 2023), is available from https://officeshock.ai. The quote about futures thinking is from *Leaders Make the Future: 10 New Skills to Humanize Leadership with Generative AI* by Bob Johansen, Jeremy Kirshbaum, and Gabe Cervantes (Berrett-Koehler Publishers, 2025). Information about *Future Library*, discussed in "Trusting a Future Library," is available from https://www.futurelibrary.no; for reporting on the project, see Richard Foster, "The Norwegian Library with Unreadable Books," *BBC Future*, June 30, 2022. In this essay I also refer to Hunter S. Thompson's *Fear and Loathing in Las Vegas: A Savage Journey to the Heart of the American Dream* (Vintage, 1989) and draw interpretations from Kevin T. McEneaney's *Hunter S. Thompson: Fear, Loathing, and the Birth of Gonzo* (Rowman & Littlefield, 2016). In "The Postdigital Library," I discuss Justin E. H. Smith's article "It's All Just Beginning," from *The Point*, March 23, 2020, and his subsequent book *The Internet is Not What You Think It Is: A History, a Philosophy, a Warning* (Princeton University Press, 2022). I mention Williams's *Stand Out of Our Light* and quote from Floridi's *The Fourth Revolution* and *The Ethics of Artificial Intelligence: Principles, Challenges, and Opportunities* (Oxford University Press, 2023).

Part Four
The Library as a Place of Action: How Libraries Are Structures for Hope

"The Library at Dawn," written after attending a silent retreat at Mount Angel Abbey in Oregon, depends on an explanation of the Divine Office by the abbey's Abbot Jeremy Driscoll. This essay draws from research I published in "The Library As Place—Really Early in the Morning," in *The Journal of the Book Club of Washington* 12:1 (2012). I quote Anne Lamott's essay "Steinbeck Country," which appears in *The Public Library*, and Dylan Thomas's "Notes on the Art of Poetry," included in *Books and Libraries: Poems*. The concept of distant reading was conceptualized by Franco Moretti in 2000; Floridi conceptualizes the concept of "distant writing" in a forthcoming essay, "Distant Writing: Literary Production in the Age of Artificial Intelligence."

In "The Archival Cycle," I quote: *Understanding Archives & Manuscripts* by James M. O'Toole and Richard J. Cox (Society of American Archivists, 2006); Paul Ricoeur's *Memory, History, Forgetting* (University of Chicago Press, 2004); Randall C. Jimerson's *Archives Power: Memory, Accountability, and Social Justice* (Society of American Archivists, 2009); and Bacon's *Works* (Taggard and Thompson, 1864). The book lifecycle comes from "A New Model for the Study of the Book" by Thomas R. Adams and Nicolas Barker, published in *A Potencie of Life: Books in Society*, edited by Barker (The British Library, 2001). An example of the records lifecycle comes from an old textbook of mine, *Information and Records Management: Document-Based Information Systems*, 4th edition, by Mary F. Robek et al. (McGraw-Hill, 1996). For more on the merging of archives and libraries, see Michael J. Paulus, Jr., "The Converging Histories and Futures of Libraries, Archives, and Museums as Seen through the Case of the Curious Collector Myron Eells," *Libraries & the Cultural Record* 46:2 (2011).

The Bradbury and Foucault quotes in "The Future of the Book" come from Anna-Sophie Springer's "Melancholies of the Paginated Mind: The Library As Curatorial Space," in *Fantasies of the Library*, edited by Anna-Sophie Springer and Etienne Turpin (MIT Press, 2016). "The New Media Library" was informed by Abby Smith Rumsey's *When We Are No More: How Digital Memory Is Shaping Our Future* (Bloomsbury, 2016) and Floridi's *Fourth Revolution*. I also refer to Neal Stephenson's novel *The Diamond Age* (Bantam Spectra, 1995) and Jenae Cohn's *Skim, Dive, Surface: Teaching Digital Reading* (West Virginia University Press, 2021). In "Library Automation and Intelligence Augmentation," I draw from a number of documents collected in *Reader in Library Services and the Computer* (National Cash Register, 1971) as well as Dennis Reynolds's *Library Automation: Issues and Applications* (R. R. Bowker, 1985) and Christine L. Borgman's "From Acting Locally to Thinking Globally: A Brief History of Library Automation," *The Library Quarterly* 67:3 (1997). For an example of how information literacy is being broadened to include AI, see Amanda Wheatley and Sandy Hervieux, "Separating Artificial Intelligence from Science Fiction: Creating an Academic Library Workshop Series on AI Literacy," in *The Rise of AI: Implications and Applications of Artificial Intelligence in Academic Libraries*, edited by Sandy Hervieux and Amanda Wheatley (Association of College and Research Libraries, 2022); for a definition of AI literacy, see Leo S. Lo, "Evaluating AI Literacy in Academic Libraries: A Survey Study with a

Focus on U.S. Employees," *College and Research Libraries* 85:5 (2024). The Ralph Parker quote, from his speech "The Machine and the Librarian," appears in C. Sean Burns's "Academic Libraries and Automation: A Historical Reflection on Ralph Halsted Parker," *portal: Libraries and the Academy* 14:1 (2014). The "on the cusp" quote comes from Brady D. Lund et al., "Perceptions toward Artificial Intelligence among Academic Library Employees," *College & Research Libraries*, July 2020. For more on the distinction between AI and IA, see John Markoff's *Machines of Loving Grace: The Quest for Common Ground Between Humans and Robots* (Ecco, 2015).

Information about the Bezos's library discussed in "From Alexandria to Alexa—and Back," comes from Julie Bort's reporting in "Jeff Bezos Explains Why the Library in His House Has Two Fireplaces with Two Inscriptions: 'Dreamers' and 'Builders,'" *Business Insider*, June 6, 2019. The advent of Alexa is discussed in Brad Stone's *Amazon Unbound: Jeff Bezos and the Invention of a Global Empire* (Simon & Schuster, 2021) and Benjamin Romano's "Five Years Ago Amazon Introduced Alexa," *Seattle Times*, November 8, 2019. On the impact of AI from the perspective of higher education, I quote from José Antonio Bowen and C. Edward Watson's *Teaching with AI: A Practical Guide to a New Era of Human Learning* (Johns Hopkins University Press, 2024). For an example of librarians helping people understand and engage with AI, see Carey Toane et al., "The 99 AI Challenge: Empowering a University Community through an Open Learning Pilot," in *The Rise of AI*.

In "The Library and Virtue," I draw from: Russell Michalak's insights in "From Ethics to Execution: The Role of Academic Librarians in Artificial Intelligence (AI) Policy-Making at Colleges and Universities" published in the *Journal of Library Administration* 63:7 (2023); Alasdair MacIntyre's *After Virtue* (Notre Dame, 2007); and Shannon Vallor's *Technology and the Virtues: A Philosophical Guide to a Future Worth Wanting* (Oxford, 2016) and *The AI Mirror*, which I quote. For a current view of new library literacies, see *Introduction to College Research* by Walter D. Butler, Aloha Sargent, and Kelsey Smith (Pressbooks, 2021). For a broad scope of what information ethics covers, see *Foundations of Information Ethics*, edited by John T. F. Burgess and Emily J. M. Knox (ALA Neal-Schuman, 2019). This essay is further developed in "Information, Automation, and Virtue: A Framework for Designing New Information Processes and Practices," in *AI and Academic Libraries: Practical Strategies for Ethical Integration, Instruction, and Innovation*, edited by Russell Michalak and Karim

Boughida and forthcoming from the Association of College and Research Libraries.

In "In and Beyond Buildings," I quote John Danaher's "Axiological Futurism: The Systematic Study of the Future of Values," *Futures* 132 (2021) and Robert Darnton's *The Case for Books: Past, Present, and Future* (PublicAffairs, 2010). Quotes in "On Enduring Institutions" are from Mary Clapinson's *A Brief History of the Bodleian Library* (The Bodleian Library, 2020). In "Finding Oneself in the Library," I quote three essays by Michel de Montaigne: "On Three Kinds of Social Intercourse," "On Books," and "On Experience," all of which are found in *The Essays of Michel de Montaigne*, translated and edited by M. A. Screech (Penguin Press, 1991). I also quote: William Shakespeare's *The Tempest*; Robert Myers's "Running on Info," *Eastside Week*, February 2, 1994; three local newspaper clippings found in the Bellevue Public Library Archives, one of which was written by Connie Beals and titled "Libraries for People as Image Change Comes"; Archibald MacLeish's "The Premise at the Center," from *Riders on the Earth: Essays and Recollections* (Houghton Mifflin, 1976); and Bowen and Watson's *Teaching with AI*. Information about the *Index Expurgatorius* comes from Smith's *Portable Magic*.

Part Five
End Matters

In "After the End," I quote from and discuss T. S. Eliot's reflections on time and death in his *Four Quartets* (Harcourt, 1971) and return to Le Guin's *Always Coming Home*. I quote from and mention the potential of AI discussed in *Genesis: Artificial Intelligence, Hope, and the Human Spirit* by Henry A. Kissinger, Craig Mundie, and Eric Schmidt (Little, Brown and Company, 2024), and I quote from Ruha Benjamin's *Race After Technology: Abolitionist Tools for the New Jim Code* (Polity, 2019) on technological challenges and opportunities. For a definition of faith, I allude to Hebrews 11:1: "faith is the assurance of things hoped for, the conviction of things not seen." The quotes in "Acknowledgments" are from *Stories of Books and Libraries*.

TOPICAL PATHWAYS AND EXPLORATIONS

For a path through this book focusing on the idea, history, and future of **the library**, read:

- 1. "Portals to Hope" for a definition of a library and its functions.
- 3. "Becoming a Librarian" on the author's experiences of the library and why he became a librarian.
- 9. "The Beginning of the Library" about the emergence of libraries in the ancient world.
- 10. "The End of a Library" on the loss and recovery of the Dead Sea Scrolls Library.
- 29. "Library Automation and Intelligence Augmentation" on how libraries have adopted and adapted new technologies in recent decades.

Questions for reflection:

1. What did you learn that was new or interesting about libraries?
2. What have been memorable library experiences in your life? What library functions have had the greatest impact on your life and how?
3. Imagine and describe your favorite or ideal library.
4. In what ways do you hope future generations will benefit from libraries?

For a pathway focusing on **defending libraries**, read:

- 15. "The Antilibrary" on what a library is not.

- 32. "In and Beyond Buildings" on the uses and values of library spaces.
- 33. "On Enduring Institutions" about why libraries have long lives.
- 34. "Finding Oneself in the Library" about how libraries change us.

Question for reflection:

1 How do different types of libraries (e.g., public and academic) support different types of library users?

2 How do you see libraries supporting their local communities?

3 What are some alternatives to libraries? What are the strengths and weaknesses of these?

4 What would a world without libraries look like?

This pathway focuses specifically on the history, meaning, and future of **the book**:

- 8. "The Beginning of the Book" about the invention of the book.
- 12. "The Industrial Imagination" on how the industrial revolutions shaped our world.
- 17. "Libraries of Babylon" on the agency of books.
- 27. "The Future of the Book" on book forms and futures.
- 28. "The New Media Library" on books and other media.

Questions for reflection:

1 Reflect on a couple of books that have had a significant impact on your life. How did they change you?

2 How did you discover books that have been important to you? When, where, and why did you read them?

3 What is your ideal reading situation like? What book forms do you prefer, and in what settings do you enjoy engaging with them? How do your preferred reading situations differ from the ways you engage with other media?

4 How can books have agency?

For a pathway focused on the idea and functions of **the archive**, read:

- 6. "Living Libraries" on the limits of the written record.
- 13. "Archival Fevers" on the meaning of archives.
- 14. "On Inexactitude in Libraries" about the limits of the archive.
- 20. "A Canticle for Libraries" on how fictional and real libraries preserve knowledge for unknown futures.
- 26. "The Archival Cycle" on the changing nature of the archive.

Questions for reflection:

1 How do you remember, revisit, or learn about the past?
2 What are limitations of archives?
3 React to the statement that the archive "opens out of the future."
4 How can libraries deepen your encounters with the past, your expectations about the future, and your experiences of the present?

To explore a key concept in this book, **attention**, read:

- 0. "On Order" for an explanation of how we experience time.
- 5. "The Emergence of Attention and Imagination" on what attention is and why it is important, especially now.
- 24. "The Postdigital Library" on the present and future integration of digital technologies into our lives.
- 25. "The Library at Dawn" on how libraries support our attention.

Questions for reflection:

1 What do you think about the most: the past, the present, or the future? How does each influence how you think about your life and the world?
2 How can libraries help you experience time?
3 Consider how your attention is challenged by technologies such as AI. How do you decide what is worthy of attention? How do you protect your attention so you can focus on those things?

4 How might you create more space for reflection before, during, or after time immersed in information? How might libraries, librarians, library spaces, or library technologies help you cultivate attention?

To explore the concepts of human and artificial **agency**, read:

- 4. "Why Libraries?" about the impact of AI on human agency.
- 7. "The City" on the development of old and new forms of artificial agency.
- 11. "The Library as a Transformative Technology" on the agency of libraries.
- 30. "From Alexandria to Alexa—and Back" on the differences between libraries and AI.
- 31. "The Library and Virtue" on the automation of tasks and the relationship between skills, ethics, and virtues.

Questions for reflection:

1 Reflect on the institutions that are most influential in your life and how they support or frustrate your goals. What institutions have values that are best aligned with your own?

2 What values or virtues are important to you as you think about your use of information?

3 Where in your life do you see good integrations of automated processes and human actions?

4 What might libraries and librarians empower you to do next?

For a path through this book focusing on **hope**, read:

- 2. "Pandemic" about hope in the midst of apocalyptic fears.
- 16. "The Apocalyptic Imagination" on uncovering fears as well as hopes.
- 19. "Promethean Hopes" on afterthoughts and forethoughts.
- 35. "After the End" on how ends are beginnings.

Questions for reflection:

1 What does the idea of hope open up for you as you imagine what is possible?
2 What resources provide you with hope and encourage you to do hopeful things?
3 Reflect on your experiences of discovery in libraries. Can you recall a time when you were surprised by something you found, which gave you a sense of hope and inspired some action?
4 React to the idea that libraries are agents of hope. What do you have the power to change, and how might a library help you?

This pathway focuses on **the future**:

- 18. "Libraries of New Atlantis" on the library as an image of a better world.
- 21. "Facing the End with Libraries" on recovering or preserving civilization through libraries.
- 22. "Library 2041" on life in 2041 and 2451, without and with libraries.
- 23. "Trusting a Future Library" about a one-hundred-year project to create a future library.

Questions for reflection:

1 What resources influence your thoughts about the future?
2 Do you think of the future as something fixed or open? Why?
3 What are your greatest fears and hopes about the future?
4 How might libraries help how you imagine and engage with the future with hope?

INDEX

Ancient Texts

Apocalypse of John (Revelation) 68–9, 71, 75, 78, 96, 131, 134, 147, 156
Dead Sea Scrolls 18, 44–6, 147, 151, 153
Epic of Gilgamesh 36–8, 40, 110, 153
Genesis 11, 27, 38, 63, 76, 78, 81, 141–2, 152, 154
Letter of Aristeas 41, 153

Libraries

Alexandria, Library of 18–19, 40–2, 63–4, 73, 87, 120
Ashurbanipal, Library of 36–7, 40, 42
Bellevue (WA) Public Library 17–18, 136, 161
Birmingham (UK) Public Library 145
Creighton University Libraries 148
Dead Sea Scrolls Library 18–19, 44–6, 153
Deichman Bibliotek, Future Library at 91–2
Gig Harbor (WA) Library v
Library of Congress 3, 7, 116, 137
Monte Cassion Library 82–3, 157
New York Public Library 94, 96
Oxford University Library 90, 131–4, 137, 147, 161
Princeton Theological Seminary Library 37, 154
Princeton University Library 102, 149
Rutgers University Library 109
Seattle Pacific University Library 148
Seattle Public Library 8, 9–11, 151
Vancouver (BC) Public Library 74
Whitman College Library 101–2, 158

People

Adams, Rachel 72, 156
Aeschylus 80, 157
Alexander, Archibald 37, 153
Asimov, Isaac 35, 84–5, 157
Aristotle 40, 42, 135
Arnold, Mary 147, 161
Atwood, Margaret 84, 91, 157
Augustine 4, 40, 150

Bacon, Francis 3–4, 75–7, 90, 94, 106, 132, 150, 156–7, 159
Becker, Paula, and Alan Stein 15, 151
Bender, Emily, and Alex Hanna 6, 150
Benedict 82, 157
Benjamin, Ruha 143, 161
Benjamin, Walter 7, 147, 150
Bezos 119–20, 132, 160
Bloch, Marc 55–6, 155
Blouin, Francis, and William Rosenberg 55, 154
Boccaccio, Giovanni 82–3, 157
Bodley, Thomas 90, 131–4
Borges, Jorge Luis 11, 57, 63, 65, 72, 155
Bowen, José Antonio, and C. Edward Watson 121, 138, 160, 161

Bradbury, Ray 71, 89, 111, 156, 159
Brueggemann, Walter 34, 152
Buechner, Frederick 31, 152

Carnegie, Andrew 49, 52-3
Cassiodorus 69, 81
Castells, Manuel 55, 155
Charlesworth, James H. 147, 151, 153
Coates, Ta-Nehisi 48, 154
Cohn, Jenae 113, 159
Cole-Turner, Ron 148, 152
Collins, John J. 46, 153, 156
Crawford, Kate 72, 156

Damrosch, David 36, 153
Danaher, John 130, 161
Dante 66, 156
Darnton, Robert 130, 161
de Bury, Richard 109, 111
de Montaigne, Michel 6, 135, 161
Derrida, Jacques 54-5, 154-5
Dick, Philip K. 44, 153
Dostoevsky, Fyodor 51-2, 154
Dove, Rita 18, 151

Eco, Umberto 17-18, 44, 151, 153
Eliot, T.S. 141, 144, 161

Floridi, Luciano 22-3, 95, 97, 114, 150, 158, 159
Foster, Richard 92, 158
Foucault, Michel 76, 111, 157, 159
Frischmann, Brett, and Evan Selinger 34, 152

Gazzaley, Adam, and Larry Rosen 28, 152

Harari, Yuval 27, 151-2
Hao, Karen 72, 156
Hay, Daisy 78, 157
Herrera, Luis 83, 157
Hilbert, Vi 31, 152
Huxley, Aldous 70, 156

James, P. D. 72, 156
Jesus 31, 44, 59, 101, 153, 156
Jimerson, Randall 104-5, 159
Johansen, Bob 89-90, 157-8
Josephus 45, 153

Kant, Immanuel 10, 150
Kissinger, Henry, Craig Mundie, and Eric Schmidt 143, 161

La Pointe, Jill 31, 152
Lamott, Anne 103, 158
Le Guin, Ursula K. 57-9, 67, 142-3, 155-6, 161
Leclercq, Jean 82, 157
Lee, Kai-Fu, and Chen Qiufan 87-9, 157
Levine, Arthur, and Scott Van Pelt 52-3, 154
Livy 41, 153

MacIntyre, Alasdair 123-4, 160
MacLeish, Archibald 137-8, 161
Mandel, Emily St. John 13-14, 151
Manguel, Alberto 72-3, 156
Mattern, Shannon 35, 152
McCarthy, Cormac 14, 151
McLuhan, Marshall 19, 51, 151, 154
Miller, Walter M. 81-3, 157
Milton, John 72, 156
Mitchell, David 91-2
Monáe, Janelle, and Alaya Dawn 64, 155-6
More, Thomas 67, 156-7

Orwell, George 70, 156
O'Toole, James, and Richard Cox 104, 159

Parker, Ralph 118, 160
Pasquale, Frank 35, 152
Paterson, Katie 91-2, 158
Plato and Socrates 30-1, 113
Porter, Noah 53, 154

Portier-Young, Anathea 45–6, 153
Purchas, Samuel 32, 152

Rayward, W. Boyd 55, 155
Ricoeur, Paul 104, 159
Rose, Jonathan 39, 153
Rumsey, Abby Smith 133, 159

Scheidel, Walter 81, 157
Schroeder, Karl 64–5, 156
Schwab, Klaus 23, 151
Seneca 41, 48, 153
Shakespeare, William 135–6, 161
Shears, Jonathon 52, 154
Shelley, Mary 68, 78–80, 156, 157
Smith, Emma 156, 161
Smith, Justin E. H. 94, 158
Springer, Anna-Sophie 111, 159
Stegemann, Hartmut 45, 153

Stephenson, Neal 76–7, 85–6, 113, 157, 159
Supp-Montgomerie, Jenna 51, 154

Thomas, Dylan 103, 158
Thompson, Hunter S. 68, 92–3, 156, 158

Vancouver, George 13, 79, 157
Vallor, Shannon 6, 49–50, 124, 150, 154, 160

Weil, Simone 29, 152
Wells, H. G. 71–2, 156
Wiegand, Wayne A. 48–9, 154
Williams, Jame 28–9, 96, 152, 158

Yang, K. Wayne 47–8, 154